# CONTENT

LASAGNE roll-ups 1-2
MUSHROOM spaghetti bolognese 3-4
OVEN-BAKED CHICKEN & mushroom risotto 5-6
SALAMI TOMATO & ricotta pizzas 7-8
CHICKEN FETTUCCINE WITH CREAMY avocado pasta sauce 9-10
EASY AVOCADO parmigiana 11-12
CHICKEN SATAY SKEWERS with gado gado 13-14
TERIYAKI BEEF noodles 15-16
KATSU PORK WITH PEAR & carrot slaw 17-18
CHICKEN & PRAWN pad Thai 19-20
SPICED SPATCHCOCK with citrus couscous 21-22
AVOCADO hummus 23-24
WARM MOROCCAN AVOCADO & ROASTED vegetable salad 25-26
MIDDLE EASTERN QUAIL & COUSCOUS SALAD WITH garlic sauce 27-28

MEXICAN spatchcock 29-30
FANTASTIC FISH tortillas 31-32
MEXICAN CHICKEN & rice casserole 33-34
BAKED BEAN & CHICKEN enchiladas 35-36
LEMONADE scones 37-38
ANZAC biscuits 39-40
HONEY joys 41-42
MELTING moments 43-44
CHOCOLATE crackles 45-46
RASPBERRY coconut slice 47-48
SPICY SCRAMBLED egg breakfast rolls 49-50
AUSSIE BUBBLE AND SQUEAK WITH FRIED egg topper 51-52
SCRAMBLED EGGS WITH star toast 53-54
CHOCOLATE POPCORN cupcakes 55-56
SPICY STRAWBERRY 57
POPCORN coconut slice 58-59

PIZZA POPCORN 60
RAMEN NOODLES with fried eggs 61-62
SUN-DRIED TOMATO, TUNA AND OLIVE Zucchini noodles 63-64
FRIED RICE with eggs 65-66
HEALTHIER CHICKEN SCHNITZEL BURGERS with avocado smash 67-68
LEMON & PEPPER CHICKEN & zucchini slaw pitas 69-70
LEMON & PEPPER CHICKEN nourish bowls 71-72
CHICKEN SCHNITZEL & EGGPLANT parmigiana 73-74
CHICKEN AND MUSHROOM FARFALLE WITH four cheese ricotta 75-76
BEEF RAVIOLI WITH THYME BURNT BUTTER and bacon 77-78
GARLIC AND HERB RICOTTA penne 79-80
GARLIC, LEMON PAN FRIED GNOCCHI WITH basil ricotta 81-82
EASY FOUR CHEESE SPAGHETTI carbonara 83-84
Mushroom BREAKFAST TARTS 85-86

ZUCCHINI FRITTERS WITH PORTABELLA Mushrooms & POACHED EGG 87-88
WAFFLES WITH SAUTEED Mushrooms & MAPLE BACON 89-90
Mushroom LAMB & FETA GOZLEME 91-92
MEDITERRANEAN Mushroom & CHORIZO SKEWERS 93-94
THE "ULTIMATE" BEEF & Mushroom BURGER 95-96
PORTABELLA Mushroom FRIES 97-98
Mushroom & LEEK FILO PIE 99-100
Mushroom VEGGIE BURGERS 101-102
Mushroom & CHAR SIU PORK STIR FRY 103-104
MAPLE ROASTED Mushroom & CARROT SALAD 105-106
Popping candy bark 107
Honey joys 108
Popcorn rocky road 109
Party snacks 110
Fun Wraps 111
Popping candy hedgehog 112
Chocolate crackle popcorn 113
Rainbow tea cake with vanilla frosting & M&M's 114

Party snacks 116
Froggy Sandwiches 117
Layered chocolate crackle slice 118
Mini red velvet cupcakes 119-120
Berry Smoothies 121
Smiley Toasts 122
Mini chocolate mudcakes 123-124
Chocolate crackles 125
Coconut ice 126
Kahlúa custard profiterole 127-128
Gluten free mini fruitcakes 129-130
Festive red velvet cupcakes 131-132
Christmas chocolate mudcake 133-134
Rum balls 135-136
Individual gluten free tiramisu 137-138
Layered chocolate crackle slice 139-140
White and dark chocolate crackles 141-142

**Tip**

Sneak chopped carrots into the mince mixture for an extra veggie hit

# LASAGNE *roll-ups*

**PREP** 20 MINS    **COOK** 50 MINS    **MAKES** 16

## INGREDIENTS

⅓ cup olive oil

500g beef mince

1 brown onion, finely diced

2 x 400g can Ardmona Diced Tomatoes

3 garlic cloves, crushed

2 tbs Italian seasoning

8 fresh lasagne sheets, cut in half, lengthways

Salt and pepper

**RICOTTA FILLING**

500g ricotta

1 egg, whisked

⅓ cup flat leaf parsley, chopped, plus extra to serve

3 ½ cups three cheese blend

## METHOD

1. Preheat oven to 180°C
2. Heat 1 tablespoon of oil in a large non-stick frying pan over medium high heat. Cook mince, breaking up with a wooden spoon. Add the onion and cook, stirring until meat is brown and onions are soft
3. Add 1 can of tomatoes, the garlic and Italian seasoning. Stir the sauce over low heat, then simmer, covered, for 10 minutes
4. Meanwhile, make the Ricotta Filling
5. Before assembling the roll-ups, evenly spread remaining can of tomatoes over the base of a 6-cup ovenproof baking dish
6. Prepare the pasta by placing the lasagne sheets in a single layer on a lined baking tray
7. Spread ¼ cup of Ricotta Filling over each of the lasagne sheets. Then spread a heaped tablespoon of the meat sauce on top
8. Roll up each filled lasagne sheet and arrange in the baking dish standing upright, nestling them together
9. Cover with any remaining meat sauce and sprinkle remaining cheese over. Carefully tent an extra long piece of aluminium foil to cover the bake, ensuring it does not touch the cheese. Bake for 30 minutes or until pasta is cooked. Remove foil and bake for a further 5 minutes to allow lasagne to turn golden and slightly crisp

**RICOTTA FILLING**

1. Put ricotta, egg, parsley, salt and pepper in a medium bowl. Add 3 cups of the cheese mix and stir to combine

### Tip
Very finely chop the mushrooms to get them past fussy eaters

# MUSHROOM
## *spaghetti bolognese*

**PREP** 15 MINS    **COOK** 45 MINS    **SERVES** 4

## INGREDIENTS

*2 tbs olive oil*

*1 brown onion, finely chopped*

*2 garlic cloves, crushed*

*2 tbs tomato paste*

*400g pork mince (see tip)*

*400g Button Mushrooms, sliced*

*2 tsp thyme leaves*

*800g can chopped tomatoes*

*400g spaghetti*

*¼ cup shredded basil leaves, plus extra whole leaves, to serve*

*Finely grated parmesan, to serve*

## METHOD

1. Heat olive oil in a large saucepan over medium heat. Add onion and garlic and cook, stirring, 5 minutes or until onion softens. Add tomato paste and cook for 1 minute

2. Add mince, increase heat to medium-high and cook, stirring, for 3-4 minutes or until browned all over. Add mushrooms and thyme and cook for a further 3 minutes

3. Add tomatoes, bring to a simmer. Season to taste. Reduce heat to low, and simmer for 30 minutes or until the sauce thickens

4. Cook spaghetti in a saucepan of boiling salted water following packet instructions. Drain and set aside

5. Add drained pasta and shredded basil to the sauce, mix well. Divide pasta between serving bowls. Serve topped with parmesan and extra basil

## TIPS & HINTS:

Bolognese can be made with any variety of mince, shop smart and check out the best buy of the week

**Top tip**

For a delicious veg only option, leave out the chicken

# OVEN-BAKED CHICKEN
## *& mushroom risotto*

**PREP** 15 MINS  **COOK** 45 MINS  **SERVES** 4

## INGREDIENTS

*2 tbs olive oil*

*500g chicken thigh fillets, cut into 3cm pieces*

*1 brown onion, finely diced*

*3 garlic cloves, finely chopped*

*250g Swiss Brown Mushrooms, sliced*

*2 cups arborio rice*

*4 cups (1L) chicken stock*

*50g baby spinach leaves*

*½ cup grated parmesan*

*Lemon wedges, to serve*

## METHOD

1. Preheat oven to 160°C fan-forced. Heat 1 tbs oil in a large ovenproof pan over medium-high heat. Brown chicken in 2 batches. Transfer to a plate. Set aside

2. Heat remaining 1 tbs oil in the pan over medium heat. Add onion and garlic. Cook, stirring often, for 3-4 minutes or until onion softens. Toss through mushrooms. Cook for 1 minute

3. Stir in rice. Cook, stirring, for 1-2 minutes or until rice is glossy. Add stock and return chicken to pan. Stir to combine and bring to the boil. Cover and bake for 25-30 minutes or until rice is just tender and liquid has almost been absorbed. Toss through spinach. Sprinkle with parmesan. Serve with lemon wedges

# SALAMI TOMATO
## & ricotta pizzas

 **PREP** 10 MINS    **COOK** 10 MINS    **SERVES** 4

Recipe uses products from brands supporting **Foodbank**

### INGREDIENTS

2 large Lebanese flatbreads

4 tbs tomato paste

2 x 80g packet Primo Thinly Sliced Danish Salami

100g grape or cherry tomatoes, halved

100g fresh ricotta, crumbled

Olive oil cooking spray

Rocket leaves & extra virgin olive oil, to serve

### METHOD

1. Preheat oven to 200°C fan-forced. Place the flatbreads onto baking trays. Spread each with 2 tbs tomato paste

2. Dividing ingredients, top each with salami, tomato and sprinkle with ricotta. Spray with oil

3. Bake for 10 minutes or until bread is crisp. Scatter with rocket. Season. Drizzle with extra virgin olive oil and serve

{ *You can also use pre-made pizza bases available from most major supermakets* }

# CHICKEN FETTUCCINE WITH CREAMY
## *avocado pasta sauce*

**PREP** 15 MINS  **COOK** 15 MINS  **SERVES** 4

## INGREDIENTS

*500g chicken breast fillets*

*2 garlic cloves*

*2 Avocados*

*½ bunch basil, leaves picked, roughly chopped*

*½ cup finely grated parmesan*

*1 lemon, finely grated rind and juice*

*¼ cup olive oil, plus extra to drizzle*

*Sea salt flakes and white pepper*

*500g cherry truss tomatoes*

*400g fettuccine pasta*

*Finely grated or shaved parmesan, to serve*

*⅓ cup small basil leaves, to serve*

## METHOD

1. Place chicken into a deep frying pan and cover with cold water. Place over a medium heat and bring to a simmer. Cook for 10 minutes. Remove from heat and cool in water. Drain chicken and shred

2. Meanwhile, place garlic, avocados, basil, parmesan, lemon rind and juice and olive oil into a food processor. Season and puree until a smooth green sauce forms

3. Preheat oven to 180°C. Line a baking tray with baking paper. Place tomatoes onto tray and drizzle with oil. Season with salt and pepper. Roast for 15 minutes or until softened

4. Cook pasta in a large saucepan of salted boiling water until just tender as per packet instructions. Drain and return to saucepan. Add shredded chicken and avocado sauce to pasta. Toss until well combined. Serve pasta topped with parmesan, basil leaves and roasted tomatoes

## Twist

We've given the Italian-Aussie parmigiana an avolicious update!

# EASY AVOCADO
## *parmigiana*

**PREP** 10 MINS    **COOK** 15 MINS    **SERVES** 4

### INGREDIENTS

*4 chicken breast fillets*

*⅓ cup plain flour*

*2 eggs, lightly whisked*

*1 cup Panko breadcrumbs*

*Olive oil, for shallow frying*

*2 tbs Dijon mustard*

*1 just-ripe Avocado, skin and seed removed, sliced*

*4 slices Swiss cheese*

### METHOD

1. Preheat oven to 200°C/180°C fan-forced. Grease and line a baking tray with baking paper
2. Place 1 chicken breast between 2 sheets of baking paper. Gently flatten with a rolling pin to ½cm thick. Repeat with remaining chicken
3. Coat each chicken breast in flour, shaking off the excess. Dip in egg, and press into breadcrumbs, coating both sides
4. Add enough oil to a non-stick frying pan to shallow fry. Heat the oil then add the chicken and fry for about 2 minutes on each side or until golden
5. Transfer to prepared tray. Evenly spread mustard over the top side of the chicken. Top with sliced avocado and then the cheese
6. Bake for 7-8 minutes or until cheese has melted and chicken is cooked through
7. Remove from oven and serve with a simple salad

**Fact**

Passage to Asia stir-fry sauces are all MSG and gluten free

# CHICKEN SATAY SKEWERS
## *with gado gado*

 **PREP** 15 MINS + MARINATING TIME    **COOK** 20 MINS    **SERVES** 4

## INGREDIENTS

*750g chicken thigh fillets, cut into 4cm cubes*

*200g Passage to Asia Satay Chicken stir-fry sauce*

*150g green beans, trimmed*

*3 cups finely shredded Savoy cabbage*

*1 carrot, finely shredded*

*1 Lebanese cucumber, thinly sliced diagonally*

*1 small red onion, thinly sliced*

*4 eggs, hard boiled, halved*

*Roasted peanuts, chopped, to serve*

## METHOD

1. Place chicken into a bowl and add Passage to Asia Satay Chicken stir-fry sauce, reserving ¼ cup to serve. Stir until well combined. Cover and marinate for 30 minutes. Thread diced chicken onto the soaked skewers

2. Meanwhile, bring a medium saucepan of water to the boil. Fill a large bowl with iced water. Cook beans for 2 minutes or until just tender. Transfer to iced water. Add cabbage to boiling water and cook for 2 minutes or until wilted. Add carrot and cook for 1 minute or until wilted. Transfer to bowl with beans.

3. Preheat oven to 180°C. Drain vegetables and place with cucumber, onion and egg onto a large platter

4. Heat a chargrill over high heat or large non-stick frying pan over medium-high heat. Line a baking tray with baking paper. Chargrill skewers for 8 minutes or until browned on all sides. Transfer to tray. Place in oven for 10 minutes or until cook through. Serve skewers with gado gado, reserved sauce, chopped peanuts

### TIPS & HINTS:
You will need to pre-soak 12 small wooden skewers

# TERIYAKI BEEF
## *noodles*

**PREP** 10 MINS    **COOK** 20 MINS    **SERVES** 4

## INGREDIENTS

*2 tbs vegetable oil*

*500g rump steak, cut into thin strips*

*1 carrot, halved lengthways, thinly sliced diagonally*

*1 red capsicum, deseeded, thinly sliced*

*1 bunch broccolini, trimmed, halved lengthways, cut into thirds*

*100g snow peas, trimmed, halved lengthways diagonally*

*4 green onions, thinly sliced diagonally*

*200g Passage to Asia Teriyaki Chicken stir-fry sauce*

*450g pkt hokkien noodles, cooked, drained*

*Toasted sesame seeds, to serve*

*Extra thinly sliced green onions, to serve*

## METHOD

1. Heat 2 tsp oil in a wok over a high heat. Cook steak in batches, for 2 minutes or until browned, adding more oil as required. Transfer to a bowl

2. Add carrot and capsicum to wok and stir-fry for 2 minutes. Add broccolini and snow peas and toss until combined. Add 2 tbs water and cook for 2 minutes or until vegetables are just softened. Return steak to wok with green onion and Passage to Asia Teriyaki Chicken stir-fry sauce. Stir until combined. Cook for 2 minutes or until heated through. Add noodles and toss to combine. Serve topped with sesame seeds and extra green onion

**Tip**

Add steamed rice for a more substantial meal

# KATSU PORK WITH PEAR
## *& carrot slaw*

 **PREP** 20 MINS    **COOK** 20 MINS   **SERVES** 4

## INGREDIENTS

*3 firm pears, quartered, cored*

*1 carrot*

*2 green onions, thinly sliced diagonally*

*2 tbs pickled pink ginger, chopped*

*¼ cup mayonnaise*

*1 lime, juiced*

*4 heart-smart pork loin medallions*

*⅓ cup plain flour*

*1 egg*

*1 cup panko breadcrumbs*

*2 tbs vegetable oil*

*20g butter*

*200g Passage to Asia Japanese Katsu Curry Sauce*

## METHOD

1. Coarsely grate pear and carrot and place in a bowl. Add onion, ginger, mayonnaise, lime juice, salt and white pepper and stir until well combined. Cover and refrigerate until required

2. Place your hand flat over a pork loin and using a sharp knife, cut through the centre from one side to the other. When almost at the other side, open pork loin out forming a thin schnitzel. Repeat with remaining pork loins

3. Place flour into a shallow bowl. Whisk egg in a shallow bowl with 1 tbs of water and place breadcrumbs into another bowl. Lightly coat schnitzels with flour, then coat with egg and breadcrumbs

4. Heat oil and butter in a large frying pan over medium heat. Cook schnitzels for 3 minutes each side or until golden and cooked through. Place Passage to Asia Japanese Katsu Curry Sauce into a small saucepan and place over a medium heat. Cook for 4 minutes or until hot. Serve schnitzel sliced and sauce spooned over with pear and carrot slaw on the side

## TIPS & HINTS:

We used Kewpie mayonnaise

# CHICKEN & PRAWN
## *pad Thai*

**PREP** 20 MINS   **COOK** 20 MINS   **SERVES** 4

## INGREDIENTS

*375g pad Thai rice noodles*

*2 tbs vegetable oil*

*16 green prawns, peeled, deveined*

*500g chicken thigh fillets, diced*

*2 eggs, whisked*

*5 green onions, thinly sliced diagonally*

*225g Passage to Asia Pad Thai stir-fry sauce*

*1 cup bean sprouts, trimmed*

*Small red chillies, thinly sliced, to serve*

*Thai basil, to serve*

## METHOD

1. Cook rice noodles as per packet instructions.

2. Heat 1 tbs oil in a hot wok. Add prawns and cook for 3 minutes or until just cooked. Transfer to a bowl. Add chicken and cook for 5 minutes or until browned and cooked through. Transfer to bowl with prawns.

3. Heat remaining oil. Add egg and cook for 1 minute or until just set. Add onion and stir until combined. Return chicken, prawns and noodles to wok with Passage to Asia Pad Thai stir-fry sauce. Toss until well combined and heated through. Remove from heat and stir in bean sprouts. Spoon into serving bowls and top with chilli and basil.

# SPICED SPATCHCOCK
## *with citrus couscous*

**PREP** 15 MINS (PLUS MARINATING TIME)   **COOK** 35 MINS   **SERVES** 4

## INGREDIENTS

**SPICE MIX**

½ red onion, roughly chopped

1 clove crushed garlic

1 tsp turmeric

2 tsp ground cumin

2 tsp paprika

¼ tsp each cayenne, sea salt and freshly ground black pepper

1 tbs fresh coriander leaves

2 tbs parsley leaves

2 tbs olive oil

4 spatchcock, backbone removed and halved

**CITRUS COUSCOUS SALAD**

1 cup instant couscous

1 cup boiling water

2 tbs extra virgin olive oil

1 small red capsicum, diced

2 tbs each of orange and lemon juice

1 tbs preserved lemon rind, finely chopped

2 tbs shredded mint

½ tsp each cinnamon and nutmeg

Greek yoghurt and extra coriander (optional), to serve

## METHOD

**SPICE MIX**

1. To make the spice mix, pound all ingredients in a mortar and pestle or process until well blended

2. Coat the spatchcock with spice mix and refrigerate for a few hours so that the flavours can develop

3. Heat the barbecue to medium and oil the bars to prevent the spatchcock from sticking. Place the spatchcocks on the grill, skin-side down, and cook for about 10 minutes each side or until juices run clear when the thigh is pierced with a sharp knife. Cover with foil and set aside for a few minutes to rest

**CITRUS COUSCOUS SALAD**

1. Place couscous in a large bowl, pour over boiling water, cover with plastic wrap and set aside for 5 minutes. Fluff up the grains with a fork then set aside for a further 5 minutes

2. Fluff again to break up any lumps. Stir together olive oil, capsicum, juices, preserved lemon, mint, cinnamon and nutmeg and pour over the couscous, toss to combine

3. Pile couscous onto plates or platter, top with spatchcock and serve with yoghurt. Garnish with extra coriander if you like.

# AVOCADO
## *hummus*

 **PREP** 10 MINS    **MAKES** 2½ CUPS

### INGREDIENTS

*400g can chickpeas, drained and rinsed*

*2 small garlic cloves, peeled*

*¼ cup firmly-packed coriander leaves*

*¼ cup extra virgin olive oil*

*2 tbs lime juice*

*1 tbs tahini*

*½ tsp ground cumin*

*2 ripe Avocados, seeds and skin removed, chopped*

*1 tbs water*

*Toasted pita bread, to serve*

### METHOD

1. In a food processor, blend chickpeas, garlic, coriander, oil and lime juice until smooth
2. Add tahini, cumin and avocados. Process again until combined, adding water if necessary for desired consistency. Season to taste
3. Serve with extra scattered chickpeas and toasted pita bread

*Top with smoked paprika to give it extra spice and a smoky flavour*

*Tip*
Add shredded roast chicken for a hearty dinner

# WARM MOROCCAN AVOCADO & ROASTED *vegetable salad*

**PREP** 20 MINS  **COOK** 30 MINS  **SERVES** 4

## INGREDIENTS

**ROASTED VEGETABLE SALAD**

*2 tbs olive oil*

*1 tsp ground cumin*

*1 tsp ground coriander*

*2 garlic cloves, crushed*

*750g orange sweet potato, peeled and cut into bite-sized pieces*

*400g (about 2 bunches) baby Dutch carrots, trimmed and peeled*

**MOROCCAN AVOCADO**

*2 just-ripe Avocados, halved and deseeded*

*100g feta cheese, crumbled*

*1 tbs lemon juice*

*2 tsp dukkah*

*50g baby spinach leaves*

*½ pomegranate, seeds removed*

*Lemon wedges and warmed flatbread, to serve*

## METHOD

**ROASTED VEGETABLE SALAD**

1. Preheat oven to 200°C/180°C fan-forced
2. Combine oil, cumin, coriander and garlic in a bowl
3. Arrange sweet potatoes and carrots in a single layer on a large baking tray lined with baking paper. Drizzle with oil mixture and toss to coat vegetables
4. Roast vegetables, turning once, for 25-30 minutes or until tender

**MOROCCAN AVOCADO**

1. Meanwhile scoop the avocado flesh into a bowl and add feta, lemon juice and sprinkle with dukkah. Gently toss to combine and set aside until the vegetables are cooked
2. To serve, arrange roasted vegetables and spinach on a serving platter. Top with avocado mixture and sprinkle with pomegranate seeds. Season to taste
3. Serve with lemon wedges and flatbread

# MIDDLE EASTERN QUAIL & COUSCOUS SALAD WITH *garlic sauce*

**PREP** 20 MINS (PLUS MARINATING TIME)  **COOK** 20 MINS  **SERVES** 4

## INGREDIENTS

**GARLIC SAUCE**

1 egg yolk
5 garlic cloves, crushed
Pinch salt
1 tbs lemon juice
100ml vegetable oil

**CORIANDER SALT**

2 tbs coriander seeds
1 tsp cumin seeds
1 tbs sea salt

**QUAIL & COUSCOUS SALAD**

400g Quail Breast Fillets
1 cup couscous
1 cup boiling water
1 Lebanese cucumber, seeds removed and diced
2 roma tomatoes, diced
½ small red onion, diced
1 x 400g can chickpeas, rinsed and drained
½ cup chopped coriander leaves
2 tbs lemon juice
2 tbs olive oil, extra for brushing

## METHOD

**GARLIC SAUCE**

1. Place egg yolk, garlic, salt and lemon into a food processor and pulse. With the food processor running, add oil in a slow steady stream until a mayonnaise forms. Set aside

**CORIANDER SALT**

1. Place spices into a dry frying pan and heat over a low heat, shaking pan, until just fragrant. Add salt and heat a further 1–2 minutes. Transfer to a plate to cool completely. Grind to a fine powder in a mortar and pestle or spice grinder

**QUAIL & COUSCOUS SALAD**

1. Rub coriander salt into quail to cover evenly and refrigerate, uncovered, for at least 1 hour

2. Place couscous into a bowl and pour over boiling water; stand for 5 minutes. Fluff couscous with a fork to separate grains. Stir through chopped vegetables, chickpeas and herbs and mix well. Whisk lemon juice and oil together and season. Stir through salad

3. Heat a chargrill or barbecue plate over medium-high heat; brush quail skin with oil and cook Breast Fillets for 3 minutes each side or until cooked to your liking

4. To serve, spoon couscous salad onto plates, top with quail and a dollop of the garlic sauce

**Top Tip**
Halve the amount of chilli powder for a milder option

# MEXICAN *spatchcock*

**PREP** 15 MINS  **COOK** 10 MINS  **SERVES** 2

## INGREDIENTS

### MEXICAN SPATCHCOCK

1 pack Game Farm deboned spatchcock (300 - 350g)

1 tsp chilli powder

½ tsp dried oregano

⅛ tsp ground cinnamon

1 garlic clove, crushed

2 tbs lemon juice

### SALSA

Chargrilled corn kernels

1 tomato, diced

1 small red onion, sliced

1 red chilli, finely chopped

Coriander leaves

Lime juice

### TO SERVE

Tortillas

Guacamole

Shredded Lettuce

## METHOD

### MEXICAN SPATCHCOCK

1. Thread each spatchcock onto a skewer
2. Combine the spices, garlic and lemon juice and brush generously over the spatchcock
3. Heat a grillpan or frypan over medium heat and cook the spatchcock for 5 minutes on each side or until cooked through

### SALSA

1. Combine salsa ingredients

### TO SERVE

1. Serve the spatchcock with salsa, tortilla, lettuce and guacamole

**Tip**
We used monkfish. Flathead would also work well

# FANTASTIC FISH *tortillas*

 **PREP** 10 MINS   **COOK** 15 MINS   **SERVES** 4

Recipe uses products from brands supporting **Foodbank**

## INGREDIENTS

**CHIPOTLE LIME CREAM**

*2 tbs chipotle sauce*

*½ cup aioli*

*1 lime, halved*

**COLESLAW**

*4 cups shredded red cabbage*

*3 shallots, thinly sliced*

*1 large carrot, shredded*

**FISH TORTILLAS**

*⅓ cup Flour*

*2 tbs Old El Paso™ Taco Spice Mix*

*600g firm white fish fillets, cut into 15cm pieces*

*Olive oil, for frying*

*1 packet Old El Paso™ Stand 'N Stuff™ Tortillas*

*Coriander, to serve*

*1 lime, halved*

## METHOD

**CHIPOTLE LIME CREAM**

1. To make the cream sauce, combine chipotle, aioli and lime juice in a medium sized bowl. Season and whisk until combined

**COLESLAW**

1. In a medium bowl, add coleslaw ingredients and mix to combine

**FISH TORTILLAS**

1. Mix the flour with the taco spice mix and use to coat the fish pieces

2. Heat oil in a non-stick frying pan over medium-high heat. Gently fry the fish in batches, cleaning the pan in between each batch and repeat until all fish is cooked. Keep warm

3. Serve tortillas filled with coleslaw, topped with fish, chipotle cream, extra coriander and a squeeze of lime

# MEXICAN CHICKEN
## & rice casserole

**PREP** 10 MINS  **COOK** 35 MINS  **SERVES** 8

Recipe uses products from brands supporting **Foodbank**

## INGREDIENTS

*1 ½ cups SunRice Medium Grain White Rice*

*3 cups chicken stock*

*425g can mexibeans*

*3 cups shredded roast chicken*

*375g jar enchilada sauce*

*250g tub sour cream*

*4 shallots, thinly sliced, plus extra for garnish*

*1½ cups cheese blend*

## METHOD

1. Preheat oven 180°C. Grease a 10 cup-capacity baking dish
2. Cook rice according to packet instructions, swapping the water for the chicken stock
3. In a medium bowl, combine cooked rice, chicken, beans, enchilada sauce, sour cream, shallots and 1 cup of the cheese. Pour into a baking dish. Cover with foil and bake for 20 minutes
4. Remove the foil and sprinkle over the remaining cheese. Return the casserole to the oven and bake for a further 5-10 minutes or until cheese is completely melted and golden
5. Top with extra shallots and serve immediately

### TIPS & HINTS:

You can spice things up by adding some chopped jalapenos on top of the casserole after baking. We used Old El Paso™ Mexe-Beans and Old El Paso™ Enchilada Sauce and Devondale Three Cheese Blend in this recipe

**tip**
Change it up and substitute chicken with stir-fried veggies

# BAKED BEAN & CHICKEN *enchiladas*

**PREP** 25 MINS    **COOK** 25 MINS    **SERVES** 4

Recipe uses products from brands supporting **Foodbank**

## INGREDIENTS

3 cups shredded roasted chicken

425g can SPC Baked Beans

2 cups Devondale Three Cheese Blend

2 tbs Old El Paso™ Fajita Spice Mix

½ cup coriander, plus extra leaves to serve

375g jar Old El Paso™ Mild Thick 'N Chunky Salsa

10 pack Old El Paso™ Regular Tortillas

Sour cream, to serve

## METHOD

1. Preheat oven to 200°C. Grease and line an ovenproof baking dish
2. In a large bowl, combine chicken with baked beans, half the cheese, fajita spice mix, coriander and 1½ cups salsa
3. Divide the mixture evenly down the centre of the tortillas (approx ⅓ cup). Roll up firmly to close and place seam-side down onto prepared baking dish. Repeat until all tortillas are filled
4. Spoon remaining salsa over the tortillas and scatter over remaining cheese
5. Bake in the oven for about 20 minutes or until cheese is melted and golden brown
6. Serve with sour cream and extra coriander leaves

## Tip

Don't overwork the dough as it may result in rock hard scones.

# LEMONADE
## *scones*

**PREP** 10-12 MINS  **COOK** 15 MINS  **MAKES** 12 SLICES

## INGREDIENTS

**LEMONADE SCONES**

*3 cups self-raising flour*

*½ tsp baking powder*

*1 tsp sugar*

*60g Copha*

*300ml lemonade*

*Plain flour, for kneading and rolling*

*1 egg, beaten*

## METHOD

1. Pre-heat oven to 190°C
2. In a large bowl, combine the self-raising flour, baking powder and sugar
3. Grate the Copha over the flour. Rub the Copha into the flour until mixture resembles fine breadcrumbs
4. Make a well in the centre of the flour mixture and pour in ¾ of the lemonade. Mix to a firm but tacky dough, adding more lemonade if required
5. Turn dough out onto a lightly floured board and knead gently
6. Roll dough out to a 4cm thick circle
7. Using a floured cutter, cut out scones. Re-roll dough as required
8. Place scones onto a floured non-stick baking tray. Brush scones with beaten egg and bake in the pre-heated oven at 190°C for 12-15 minutes
9. Cool on a wire rack and serve warm

## TIPS & HINTS:

If making date or sultana scones, add ½ cup of fruit and 1 beaten egg to the mixture

# ANZAC *biscuits*

**PREP** 15 MINS    **COOK** 12 MINS    **MAKES** 18 BISCUITS

## INGREDIENTS

*125g (½ block) Fairy margarine*
*3 tbs golden syrup*
*½ tsp bicarb soda*
*2 tbs hot water*
*150g (1 cup) plain flour, sifted*
*110g (½ cup) caster sugar*
*90g (1 cup) desiccated coconut*
*90g (1 cup) rolled oats*

## METHOD

1. Pre-heat oven to 150°C. Line 2 baking trays with baking paper
2. Melt Fairy and golden syrup in a small saucepan over low heat. Add the bicarb soda mixed with water
3. Combine the dry ingredients in a large mixing bowl, pour melted Fairy mixture into the centre and mix together
4. Roll heaped tablespoons of the mixture and place on the prepared trays. Flatten the mix down with the palm of your hand until approx. 1cm
5. Bake for 10–12 minutes or until golden brown. Cool on a cooling rack

*Tip*

Store in an airtight container for up to 3 days

> **ADD SULTANAS, DRIED CRANBERRIES OR CHOCOLATE CHIPS FOR EXTRA GOODNESS**

# HONEY *joys*

 **PREP** 8-10 MINS   **COOK** 15 MINS   **MAKES** 18 HONEY JOYS

## INGREDIENTS

*60g Copha*

*2 tbs honey*

*⅓ cup sugar*

*4 cups corn flakes*

## METHOD

1. Pre-heat oven 150°C
2. Melt together the Copha, honey and sugar in a saucepan over low heat, stirring until the sugar has dissolved. Allow mixture to cool slightly
3. Place the corn flakes into a large mixing bowl, then pour the Copha mixture over. Mix well to coat flakes
4. Spoon the honey joy mixture into muffin trays lined with paper cases
5. Bake the honey joys in the pre-heated oven at 150°C for 10 minutes
6. Remove tray from oven and cool on a wire rack. Honey joys will firm on cooling
7. When cool, store in an airtight tin

## TIPS:

These honey joys are gluten free

**Tip**

Mix up the flavour by using a different jam variety

# MELTING *moments*

**PREP** 20 MINS  **COOK** 12 MINS  **MAKES** 10 BISCUITS

## INGREDIENTS

### BISCUITS

*125g (½ block) Fairy margarine, softened*

*75g (½ cup) icing sugar, sifted*

*½ tsp vanilla essence*

*100g (⅔ cup) plain flour, sifted*

*75g (½ cup) cornflour, sifted*

### ORANGE CREAM

*60g (¼ block) Fairy margarine, softened*

*160g (1 cup) icing sugar, sifted*

*1 tsp grated orange rind*

*½ tbs orange juice*

### ASSEMBLY

*Raspberry jam, to serve*

*Icing sugar, to dust*

## METHOD

### BISCUITS

1. Preheat oven to 160°C. Line baking trays with baking paper
2. Cream Fairy, icing sugar and vanilla together until light and fluffy. Add flour and cornflour and mix well
3. Roll heaped teaspoons of mixture into balls and place on the prepared trays. Flatten with the back of a fork to make an indent
4. Bake in oven for 10-12 mins until golden

### ORANGE CREAM

1. Beat Fairy until smooth. Gradually add icing sugar. Beat until light and creamy
2. Add the rind and juice, and beat until combined

### ASSEMBLY

1. Sandwich 2 biscuits together with the orange filling and some raspberry jam
2. Dust with icing sugar

{ *For white chocolate crackles, substitute the cocoa powder with milk powder and add 200g white chocolate* }

# CHOCOLATE *crackles*

 **PREP** 10 MINS (PLUS SETTING TIME)　 **COOK** 5 MINS　 **MAKES** 12

## INGREDIENTS

*250g (1 block) Copha*

*125g (1 cup) icing sugar*

*60g (½ cup) cocoa powder*

*4 cups Rice Bubbles*

*100g (1 cup) desiccated coconut*

## METHOD

1. Line a standard 12 cup muffin tray with paper cases.
2. Melt Copha in microwave on high or in a saucepan until fully melted. Mix Rice Bubbles, icing sugar, cocoa powder and desiccated coconut in a large bowl. Add in the melted Copha, and stir to combine.
3. Spoon crackle mix evenly into the prepared muffin cups. Place in fridge for 1 hour to set.

" CHOCOLATE CRACKLES AREN'T JUST FOR PARTIES, ADD TO LUNCH BOXES FOR A GLUTEN-FREE TREAT.

# RASPBERRY
## *coconut slice*

**PREP** 10 MINS  **COOK** 20 MINS  **MAKES** 12 SLICES

## INGREDIENTS

### BASE

*125g (½ block) Fairy margarine, softened*

*110g (½ cup) caster sugar*

*1 egg*

*225g (1½ cups) self-raising flour, sifted*

### TOPPING

*90g (1 cup) desiccated coconut*

*110g (½ cup) caster sugar*

*1 egg*

*½ tsp vanilla essence*

*2 tbs raspberry jam*

## METHOD

### BASE

1. Preheat oven to 180°C. Line a 20cm square sandwich tin with baking paper
2. Cream Fairy and sugar together until light and fluffy. Beat in the egg and fold into the flour
3. Press the mixture into prepared tin

### TOPPING

1. Combine coconut, sugar, egg and vanilla together, mix well
2. Spread the raspberry jam over the base and spread the coconut mixture evenly over the top
3. Place into the oven and bake for 15-20 minutes or until golden brown
4. Cool in tin and cut into squares

# SPICY SCRAMBLED
## *egg breakfast rolls*

**PREP** 10 MINS   **COOK** 6-8 MINS   **SERVES** 4

## INGREDIENTS

*4 x 15cm pieces French bread stick (or use 4 long bread rolls)*

*¼ cup peri peri spicy mayonnaise*

*6 large eggs, at room temperature*

*⅓ cup milk*

*½ tsp dried chilli flakes*

*2 tbs butter, chopped*

*60g rocket leaves*

## METHOD

1. Halve bread and spread cut sides with mayonnaise
2. Use a fork to whisk eggs, milk and chilli flakes in a bowl until just combined. Set aside for a few minutes to allow foam to settle
3. Heat a medium non-stick frying pan over medium heat. Add butter, melt and swirl to coat pan base. Add egg mixture and cook without stirring for 30 seconds
4. Using a wide spatula, push the set eggs around outer edge toward the centre of the pan, tilting the pan to allow the uncooked egg to run over the base. Gently push eggs around pan every 15 seconds until soft folds form and one quarter mixture is unset. Remove from heat
5. Gently fold the egg mixture once more. Divide scrambled eggs and rocket between bread. Season and serve

**Tip**

This is a great dish for using up those leftover veggies

# AUSSIE BUBBLE AND SQUEAK WITH FRIED
## *egg topper*

**PREP** 10MINS  **COOK** 15 MINS  **SERVES** 2

### INGREDIENTS

*1 tbs olive oil + cooking oil spray*

*500g leftover roasted vegetables (such as sweet potato, pumpkin, potato and carrots), roughly chopped*

*1 cup frozen peas*

*2 eggs, at room temperature*

### METHOD

1. Heat oil in a medium non-stick frying pan over medium heat. Add roasted vegetables and cook, tossing often, for 4-5 minutes until vegetables are hot and crisp at the edges. Toss through peas and keep warm over low heat

2. Spray a separate medium non-stick frying pan with oil to grease. Heat over medium heat. Crack eggs into pan and fry until cooked to your liking. Top vegetables with fried eggs, season and serve

**tip**

This recipe is great for fussy kids as they can't resist the star shaped toast!

# SCRAMBLED EGGS WITH *star toast*

**PREP** 5 MINS  **COOK** 10 MINS  **SERVES** 2

## INGREDIENTS

*4 eggs, lightly beaten*

*2 tbsp full cream milk or cream*

*15g Western Star Spreadable, plus extra for toast*

*4 thick slices white, brown or multigrain bread*

## METHOD

1. Place the eggs and milk into a medium bowl and season with salt and pepper. Whisk until frothy
2. Melt Western Star Spreadable in a medium non-stick frying pan over a medium heat. Once melted, add the eggs, and stir gently with a wooden spoon for 2 minutes or until the eggs are just set. Remove the pan from the heat
3. Place the slices of bread in the toaster, and toast until golden. Once toasted, spread with Western Star Spreadable, and then get the kids to help you use a cookie cutter to cut into star shapes
4. Serve the eggs immediately with the star toast

# Treats

The perfect blend of salty and sweet

# CHOCOLATE POPCORN *cupcakes*

**PREP** 15 MINS · **COOK** 10 MINS · **SERVES** 12

## INGREDIENTS

**BASE**

½ cup coconut oil, melted

¼ cup coconut sugar

¼ cup desiccated coconut

1 cup hazelnut meal or almond meal

⅓ cup rolled oats

2 tablespoons cacao

**FILLING**

1 cup nut butter of choice

½ cup coconut oil, melted and slightly cooled

3 tablespoons agave nectar

1 teaspoon vanilla extract

4 cups Sea Salt Popcorn

**TOPPING**

2 tablespoons coconut oil, melted and cooled

1-2 tablespoons cacao

## METHOD

**BASE**

1. Pre-heat oven to 180°C or 160°C fan forced. Line a standard 12-hole muffin tin with muffin cases
2. Combine base ingredients in a medium bowl and divide evenly between prepared muffin cases. Gently press into cases to flatten
3. Bake for 10 minutes, remove from oven and cool

**FILLING**

1. Combine all filling ingredients in a medium bowl. Pour over cooled bases pressing in gently to secure

**TOPPING**

1. Add topping ingredients to a small bowl and whisk to combine
2. Using a spoon, drizzle over the top of the popcorn then place in the fridge for 1 hour or until set

# SPICY STRAWBERRY
## *and jalapeno salsa*

**PREP** 15 MINS  **SERVES** 4

### INGREDIENTS

2-3 x 250g punnets strawberries (about 20 strawberries) washed and hulled

½ Spanish onion, finely diced

1 jalapeno, chopped

¼ cup coriander chopped

Juice of 1 lime (about 1 tbsp)

Freshly cracked black pepper

168g packet Cobs By the Sea Salt Naked Corn Chips

### METHOD

1. Dice the strawberries into small pieces. Then, combine remaining ingredients in a medium bowl. Toss well

2. Serve immediately with Cobs By the Sea Salt Naked Corn Chips

# POPCORN
## *coconut slice*

**PREP** 5 MINS  **COOK** 5 MINS  **SERVES** 10-12

### INGREDIENTS

⅓ cup honey

30g butter

5 Medjool dates, pitted and chopped

120g packet Lightly Salted, Slightly Sweet Popcorn

½ cup pecans, chopped

⅓ cup mixed fruit & nuts (we used Goji Berry Super mix) plus extra for on top

### METHOD

1. Grease and line a lamington pan
2. Combine the popcorn, pecans and berry/nut mix in a medium bowl
3. Heat honey, butter and dates in a small saucepan over medium heat, stirring until melted
4. Pour into the popcorn bowl and stir to combine
5. Press into prepared lamington pan, sprinkle with extra berries, nuts and coconut. Chill 30 minutes or until firm. Slice into portions

*Tip: This popcorn slice can be whipped up in 10 minutes*

# PIZZA POPCORN

**PREP** 5 MINS  **COOK** 10 MINS  **SERVES** 4

## INGREDIENTS

80g packet Sea Salt Popcorn
40g butter, softened
1 tablespoon pizza sauce
2 teaspoon Tuscan seasoning
1 teaspoon paprika
1 teaspoon garlic powder
1 teaspoon oregano

## METHOD

1. Pre-heat oven to 180°C/160°C fan forced, grease and line 2 oven trays
2. Grease and line 2 oven trays
3. Combine butter, spices and pizza sauce
4. Put popcorn into a large bowl, add the butter and spices. Stir to combine
5. Spread onto the trays evenly in a single layer. Bake for 10 minutes, stirring half way through
6. Remove from oven and pour into a bowl and serve

## tip
A twist on the traditional, try with fried egg instead

# RAMEN NOODLES
## *with fried eggs*

**PREP** 5 MINS　**COOK** 5 MINS　**SERVES** 2

## INGREDIENTS

*2 x 120g packs ramen noodles*
*½ cup frozen peas*
*100g red capsicum, chopped*
*2 tablespoons soy sauce*
*1 teaspoon sesame oil*
*3 green onions, sliced*
*4 fried eggs*

## METHOD

1. Cook the ramen noodles according to packet instructions. Two minutes before draining, add the peas and capsicum and continue simmering with the noodles, then drain, reserving one tablespoon cooking liquid and return to the pan

2. To serve, toss the combined soy, sesame oil and cooking liquid through the noodles along with the green onions and divide between bowls. Serve topped with fried eggs and a sprinkle of dried chilli if desired

**Tip**
keep the carbs low and use fresh zucchini noodles

# SUN-DRIED TOMATO, TUNA AND OLIVE
## *zucchini noodles*

 PREP 5 MINS   COOK 5 MINS   SERVES 2

## INGREDIENTS

*250g Ricotta Pasta Stir through, Sundried Tomato*

*2 spring (green) onions, trimmed and thinly sliced*

*⅓ cup pitted Kalamata olives*

*500g fresh spiralised zucchini noodles (see note)*

*185g can tuna in olive oil, drained and roughly flaked*

*Salt and pepper, to taste*

*⅓ cup small basil leaves*

*Perfect Italiano parmesan, finely grated, to serve*

## METHOD

1. Heat a lar e non-stick fr ing pan over medium to low heat. Add  Ricotta Pasta Stir-through, Sundried Tomato, spring onions and olives. Gently stir to combine and heat until hot

2. Gently toss through zucchini noodles. Add tuna, season to taste. Sprinkle with basil and parmesan. Serve with a leafy salad if desired

### NOTE
*Spiralised zucchini noodles are available in the fresh produce section in most large supermarkets. To make 500g spiralised zucchini noodles, you'll need about 600g zucchini. Spiralise the zucchini using a spiraliser or julienne peeler to create long thin ribbons.*

*Tip*

You can use leftover rice in this recipe

# FRIED RICE
## *with eggs*

 **PREP** 10 MINS    **COOK** 15 MINS   **SERVES** 4

### INGREDIENTS

*8 eggs, medium hard boiled*

*2 tablespoons canola oil*

*115g punnet baby corn, halved lengthways*

*100g snow peas, trimmed and halved*

*1 clove garlic, crushed*

*2 teaspoons finely grated ginger*

*2 cups shredded Chinese cabbage*

*4 cups cooked long grain rice*

*⅓ cup soy sauce*

*4 green onions, sliced*

*½ cup bean sprouts, trimmed*

### METHOD

1. Heat the oil in a wok or large deep frying pan over medium heat
2. Cook the baby corn for 1-2 minutes then add the snow peas, garlic and ginger. Cook for another 1-2 minutes until tender
3. Toss the cabbage in the wok, cook for a minute until starting to wilt then stir in the rice and cook for 4-5 minutes until heated through
4. Stir the soy through the rice, and cook for another 2-3 minutes, moving the rice around the wok to mix in with the soy evenly
5. To serve, cut the egg into thick slices. Divide the rice between serving bowls and top with egg, a scatter of green onions and bean sprouts

# HEALTHIER CHICKEN SCHNITZEL BURGERS
## *with avocado smash*

**PREP** 15 MINS  **COOK** 25 MINS  **SERVES** 4

## INGREDIENTS

400g Free Range Herb Ciabatta Chicken Schnitzels

½ cup reduced fat Greek-style natural yoghurt

2 tablespoons medium peri peri sauce

4 sourdough or seeded bread rolls, halved

4 small ice-berg lettuce leaves

2 Lebanese cucumbers, thinly sliced lengthways

Sweet potato fries, to serve

**Avocado smash**

1 large ripe avocado

1 tablespoon lemon juice

75g feta, crumbled

## METHOD

1. Cook free range herb ciabatta chicken schnitzels following packet directions.

2. Meanwhile, to make avocado smash, halve avocado lengthways, remove the seed and roughly chop. Place into a bowl. Add lemon juice and season with salt and pepper. Roughly mash with a fork. Stir through feta. Set aside.

3. Combine yoghurt and peri peri sauce in a small bowl until smooth. Set aside.

4. Toast bread rolls. Divide avocado smash between bread rolls. Top roll bases with lettuce and cucumber. Halve schnitzels. Top each burger with a schnitzel. Drizzle with peri peri yoghurt and top with roll tops. Serve with remaining peri peri yoghurt and sweet potato fries.

# LEMON & PEPPER CHICKEN
## *& zucchini slaw pitas*

 **PREP** 15 MINS    **COOK** 20 MINS    **SERVES** 4

## INGREDIENTS

*350g Free Range Lemon & Pepper Chicken Tenders*

*4 pita pocket breads*

*Extra kewpie mayonnaise and lemon wedges, to serve*

**Zucchini slaw**

*250g packet fresh zucchini noodles*

*1 carrot, grated*

*3 cups finely shredded Savoy cabbage*

*½ small red onion, very thinly sliced*

*¼ cup Kewpie mayonnaise*

## METHOD

1. Cook frozen lemon & pepper chicken tenders following packet directions. Warm pita breads in the oven in the last few minutes of the chicken cooking

2. Meanwhile, to make zucchini slaw, cook zucchini noodles following packet directions. Rinse in cold water and set aside to drain. Wrap zucchini noodles in paper towel and squeeze out excess water Combine zucchini noodles, carrot, cabbage and onion in a bowl. Season with salt and pepper. Add mayonnaise and toss to combine

3. Halve chicken tenders lengthways. Halve pita breads and fill each halved pita bread with zucchini slaw and chicken tenders. Serve with extra mayonnaise and lemon wedges

**Tip**

When slicing the Brussels sprouts, keep any leaves that fall off and add to the pan

# LEMON & PEPPER CHICKEN
## *nourish bowls*

**PREP** 15 MINS   **COOK** 20 MINS   **SERVES** 4

## INGREDIENTS

2 x 350g Free Range Lemon & Pepper Chicken Tenders

1 tablespoon olive oil

500g small Brussels sprouts, finely sliced lengthways

2 spring onions, trimmed and thinly sliced

2 garlic cloves, finely chopped

450g pkt 2 ½-minute brown rice

⅓ cup pepitas

⅓ cup flaked natural almonds

200g snow peas, trimmed and blanched

Mint leaves and lemon wedges, to serve

**Tahini yoghurt dressing**

½ cup Greek-style natural yoghurt

1 tablespoon tahini

1 tablespoon lemon juice

## METHOD

1. Cook frozen Lemon & Pepper Chicken Tenders following packet directions

2. Meanwhile, to make tahini yoghurt dressing, place all ingredients in a small bowl. Season with salt and pepper. Mix until combined. Set aside

3. Heat oil in a large frying pan over medium-high heat. Add sprouts, green onions and garlic. Cook, tossing often, for 4-5 minutes until just tender. Reduce heat and keep warm

4. Cook rice in the microwave following packet directions. Place into a bowl. Toss through half of the pepitas and almonds. Set remaining pepitas and almonds aside

5. Divide rice mixture, sprouts and snow peas among shallow serving bowls. Slice chicken lengthways and add to bowls. Drizzle with tahini yoghurt dressing. Scatter with remaining pepitas and almonds. Sprinkle with mint leaves and serve with lemon wedges

# CHICKEN SCHNITZEL & EGGPLANT
## *parmigiana*

 **PREP** 15 MINS   **COOK** 30 MINS  **SERVES** 4

## INGREDIENTS

400g Free Range Herb Ciabatta Chicken Schnitzels

Olive oil, for shallow frying

400g eggplant, cut into 1cm thick rounds

500g jar tomato pasta sauce

180g tub bocconcini, drained and torn

Basil leaves, steamed broccolini and crusty bread, to serve

## METHOD

1. Cook free range herb ciabatta chicken schnitzels following packet directions, for 15 minutes (instead of 25 minutes as per packet directions)

2. Meanwhile, heat ½ cm oil in a large frying pan over medium-high heat. Cook eggplant, in 2 batches (adding extra oil as needed), for 3-4 minutes on each side until golden. Drain on paper towel

3. Pour tomato sauce into a heatproof bowl, cover and heat in the microwave on high for 1-2 minutes until hot and bubbling

4. Pour two thirds of the hot tomato sauce into a 6-cup (about 5cm deep) baking dish. Arrange eggplant and schnitzels in sauce. Drizzle with the remaining tomato sauce and scatter with bocconcini. Bake at 180°C fan-forced for 12-15 minutes until bocconcini begins to melt. Scatter with basil leaves. Serve with steamed broccolini and crusty bread

### Tip
Chicken and mushrooms are a classic pasta dinner combination

# CHICKEN AND MUSHROOM FARFALLE WITH *four cheese ricotta*

**PREP** 7 MINS  **COOK** 14 MINS  **SERVES** 4

## INGREDIENTS

*500g farfalle*

*1 tbsp. olive oil*

*2 skinless chicken breasts, chopped into 2cm pieces*

*250g button or swiss brown mushrooms, sliced*

*450g Ricotta Pasta Stir Through, Four Cheese*

*Salt and Pepper to taste*

*⅓ cup parsley finely chopped to garnish*

## METHOD

1. Cook pasta according to packet instructions
2. Meanwhile, add olive oil to a large pan and place over medium to high heat. Once hot add the chicken and mushrooms and fry until cooked and golden. Turn heat to low and add drained cooked pasta to the pan
3. Add Ricotta Pasta Stir Through Four Cheese to the pot and gently stir through
4. Once warmed through, season to taste and garnish with parsley

ADD A LITTLE WATER IF YOU WANT YOUR SAUCE A BIT THINNER

# BEEF RAVIOLI WITH THYME BURNT BUTTER
## *and bacon*

 **PREP** 10 MINS   **COOK** 20 MINS   **SERVES** 2

## INGREDIENTS

*375g packet of beef ravioli*

*80g Original Butter*

*3 rashers middle bacon, chopped*

*3 sprigs thyme, leaves picked*

*2 cloves garlic, finely chopped*

*1 handful baby spinach, washed*

*Salt and pepper, to taste*

*½ cup Perfect Italiano Parmesan, shaved*

## METHOD

1. Cook the ravioli according to packet instructions. Drain into a colander

2. While the pasta is cooking, add the butter to a large frying pan over a medium heat. When the butter melts and starts to foam, add the bacon and fry until golden brown

3. Add the thyme and garlic and continue to fry for another minute. Turn off the heat and stir through the spinach and pasta. Season with salt and pepper

4. Serve the pasta with Shaved Parmesan on top

easy vegetarian

# GARLIC AND HERB RICOTTA
## *penne*

**PREP** 5 MINS  **COOK** 18 MINS  **SERVES** 4

## INGREDIENTS

*500g penne*

*1 tbsp. olive oil*

*1 medium red onion, cut into thin wedges*

*½ tsp dried chilli flakes*

*400g tomato medley or cherry tomatoes*

*450g Ricotta Pasta Stir through, Garlic & Herb*

*Salt and pepper, to taste*

*⅓ cup basil leaves*

*Grated Parmesan, finely grated, to serve*

## METHOD

1. Cook pasta according to packet instructions
2. Meanwhile, heat olive oil in a large frying pan over medium to high heat. Add the onion and fry, stirring often, until almost tender. Add chilli flakes and tomatoes and fry, stirring often, until tomatoes are hot and softening
3. Reduce heat to low and add the drained cooked pasta. Add Ricotta Pasta Stir Through, Garlic & Herb and gently stir until well combined and hot. Season to taste, scatter with basil leaves and serve with grated parmesan

*Top Tip*

Fry your veggies in butter for a caramelised flavour

# GARLIC, LEMON PAN FRIED GNOCCHI WITH
## *basil ricotta*

**PREP** 5 MINS  **COOK** 12 MINS  **SERVES** 4

## INGREDIENTS

*2 sprigs basil, shredded*

*200g Ricotta*

*500g gnocchi*

*150g Original Salted Butter*

*2 garlic cloves, chopped*

*½ onion, diced*

*40g pine nuts*

*1 sprig parsley & thyme, chopped*

*1 lemon (zest & juice)*

*100g spinach*

*Salt & pepper*

## METHOD

1. In a bowl combine the basil and Ricotta, check seasoning
2. Cook gnocchi according to packet instructions, strain and allow to dry for a moment
3. Heat a lare an over a medium heat, add ½ the  butter, garlic, onion, pine nuts and gnocchi to the pan, and caramelise for 5 minutes on all sides
4. Add the chopped herbs, lemon zest, spinach and remaining butter, then increase heat for 1 minute
5. Remove the pan from heat, and season with salt and pepper
6. Serve the gnocchi with a generous sprinkle of Parmesan, dollops of the basil ricotta combination and a squeeze of lemon

**Tip**

Family favourite carbonara without the cream!

# EASY FOUR CHEESE SPAGHETTI
## *carbonara*

**PREP** 5 MINS **COOK** 18 MINS **SERVES** 4

### INGREDIENTS

*500g spaghetti*

*1 tbsp olive oil*

*200g short-cut bacon rashers, chopped*

*450g Perfect  Pasta Stir Through, Four Cheese*

*Salt and pepper, to taste*

*½ cup flat-leaf parsley leaves, roughly chopped*

* Parmesan, finely grated, to serve*

### METHOD

1. Cook pasta according to packet instructions. Once cooked, drain, reserving a small amount of pasta water

2. Meanwhile, heat olive oil in the large non-stick frying pan over medium to high heat. Add bacon and fry, stirring often, until crispy

3. Reduce heat to low and add the cooked  asta and pasta water. Add Perfect         Pasta Stir Through, Four Cheese and gently stir until well combined and hot

4. Season to taste,  entl  toss throu h the parsley. Serve with              Parmesan

" ENJOY A CREAMY TEXTURE WITHOUT THE CALORIES BY USING RICOTTA

*Much* **BETTER BREAKFAST**

# Mushroom
# BREAKFAST TARTS

**Prep: 10 mins   Cook: 15 mins   Serves: 6**

## Ingredients

- 2 tbsp olive oil
- 200g Button Mushrooms, trimmed and quartered
- 4 (100g) bacon rashers, trimmed and chopped (1cm pieces)
- 1 red capsicum, finely chopped
- 2 tbsp chopped thyme leaves, plus sprigs to garnish
- 3 sheets puff pastry
- 6 eggs

## Method

1. Heat oil in a large frying pan over medium high heat. Cook mushrooms for 4-5 minutes or until golden. Add bacon and thyme and cook for 2-3 minutes or until bacon is crisp. Add capsicum, cook for 2 minutes

2. Preheat oven to 200°C fan forced. Lightly grease 6 x 10.5cm (base) loose base fluted tart tins. Using a 14cm cutter, cut 6 rounds from the pastry. Line pans with pastry, prick well with a fork and trim the edges

3. Place tins on a baking tray and cook for 15 minutes or until pastry is just golden. When cool enough to touch, gently push pastry down into the base

4. Break an egg into each pastry shell, top with mushroom mixture. Cook in oven for 10-12 minutes or until egg white is cooked and yolk is slightly runny. Serve with thyme sprigs to garnish

## *Much* BETTER BREAKFAST

# ZUCCHINI FRITTERS WITH PORTABELLA *Mushrooms* & POACHED EGG

**Prep:** 10 mins  **Cook:** 15 mins  **Serves:** 4  **Makes:** 8 Fritters

## Ingredients

- 4 (240g) Portabella Mushrooms, thickly sliced
- 50g butter
- 240g truss cherry tomatoes, cut into 4 lengths
- ¾ cup olive oil
- 350g zucchini, grated
- 100g halloumi cheese, chopped
- 1 tsp sweet paprika
- 2 green onions, thinly sliced
- 6 eggs
- ½ cup (75g) self raising flour
- ⅓ cup (75ml) milk

## Method

1. Heat butter in a large saucepan over medium heat. Once melted, add mushrooms and cook for 5 minutes or until tender and lightly browned. Remove mushrooms and set aside
2. Meanwhile, preheat oven to 180°C fan forced. Line a baking tray with baking paper. Place cherry tomatoes on the baking tray and drizzle with 2 tablespoons olive oil. Season with salt and pepper. Cook for 10-12 minutes or until tomatoes have softened
3. Using hands squeeze zucchini to remove any excess liquid. Combine zucchini, halloumi, paprika and green onion in a medium bowl. Season with salt and pepper. Combine flour, 2 eggs and milk in a separate bowl. Add zucchini mixture and stir gently until combined
4. Heat 1/3 of the oil in a large frying pan over medium heat. Drop 1/4 cup of the fritter mixture into a pan and cook, in batches, for 5 minutes each side or until cooked through
5. Meanwhile, poach remaining 4 eggs in a pan of simmering water for 4-5 minutes or until cooked to your liking
6. Place zucchini fritters on plate, top with mushrooms, poached egg and cherry tomatoes to serve

*Much* **BETTER BREAKFAST**

# WAFFLES WITH SAUTEED *Mushrooms* & MAPLE BACON

**Prep: 10 mins  Cook: 15 mins  Serves: 4**

## Ingredients

- 8 (200g) rashers streaky bacon
- ¼ cup maple syrup
- 1 egg, separated
- 1 tbsp caster sugar
- ¾ cup (175ml) milk
- 80g butter, melted
- 1 cup (140g) self-raising flour
- 400g Swiss Brown Mushrooms, halved
- 2 tbsp chives, sliced
- Sour cream and chives to serve

## Method

1. Preheat oven to 180°C fan-forced. Line a baking tray with baking paper
2. Place bacon in a single layer and brush with maple syrup. Cook for 20 minutes or until crisp
3. Place egg yolk, milk, 60g melted butter and flour together in a medium bowl and whisk to combine. Whisk egg whites and sugar in a small bowl until light and fluffy and gently fold into flour mixture
4. Preheat a waffle iron. Use 1/4 cup of the waffle batter at a time. Cook for 4 minutes or until golden
5. Melt remaining butter in a large frying pan over medium high heat. Add mushrooms and chives. Season with salt and pepper. Cook, stirring occasionally for about 5 minutes or until mushrooms are lightly golden
6. Place waffles on serving plates. Top with maple bacon, mushrooms, sour cream and chives

*Much* **EASIER ENTERTAINING**

# Mushroom LAMB & FETA GOZLEME

**Prep: 25-40 mins    Cook: 6 mins    Serves: 4**

## Ingredients

| | |
|---|---|
| 1 tsp caster sugar | 400g lamb mince |
| ½ cup (125ml) warm water | 1 tsp ground cumin |
| 2 tsp dried yeast | 1 tsp dried oregano |
| 3 cups (420g) plain flour | ½ cup (20g) flat leaf parsley, chopped |
| ½ tsp salt | ½ cup (20g) mint leaves, chopped |
| ½ cup (125ml) warm milk | 200g Button Mushrooms, sliced |
| 2 tbsp olive oil | 200g feta, crumbled |
| 1 brown onion, thinly sliced | Lemon wedges, to serve |
| 1 garlic clove, crushed | |

## Method

1. Combine sugar, water and yeast in a jug. Stand for 10 minutes
2. Place flour and salt in a large bowl. Add yeast mixture and milk and combine to make a soft dough. Turn onto a lightly floured board and knead gently until smooth. Divide dough into four portions. Place on a lightly floured board, cover with plastic and stand in a warm place for 20 minutes or until dough has doubled in size
3. Meanwhile, heat half of the oil in a large non-stick frying pan over medium heat. Add onion and garlic and cook, stirring often for 5 minutes or until onion is soft
4. Increase the heat to high, add mince, cumin and oregano and cook, stirring to break up the lumps, for 10 minutes until browned. Transfer to a bowl. Cool for 5 minutes, add parsley and mint
5. Heat remaining oil in same frying pan. Add the mushrooms and cook a further 5 minutes or until browned lightly. Remove from heat
6. On a lightly floured surface roll dough into a 30cm x 40cm rectangle. Place one-quarter of the mince mixture, mushrooms and feta on one half of each rectangle. Season with salt and pepper. Fold dough over to enclose filling. Press edges together to seal
7. Preheat a barbecue plate or frying pan on medium until hot
8. Brush both sides of dough with oil and cook for about 3 minutes or until golden, then turn and cook for a further 3 minutes. Serve with lemon wedges

# MEDITERRANEAN Mushroom & CHORIZO SKEWERS

**Cook: 8 mins    Serves: 4**

## Ingredients

3 tbs extra virgin olive oil

1 lemon, juiced

2 tsp smoked paprika

2 tsp brown sugar

24 button mushrooms

3 chorizo sausages (see tip)

1 red capsicum

1 yellow capsicum

Tossed salad & lemon wedges, to serve

## Method

1. Combine oil, lemon juice, paprika and sugar in a large bowl, season with salt and pepper and whisk until well combined. Add the mushrooms and stir to coat all the mushrooms. Cover and refrigerate for 1 hour to marinate

2. Cut each chorizo into 8 slices. Cut capsicums into pieces. Thread the chorizo, capsicum and mushrooms alternately onto 8 skewers

3. Heat a lightly greased barbecue plate on medium-high. Barbecue the skewers, turning often, for 6-8 minutes or until mushrooms and chorizo are warmed through. Serve with salad and lemon wedges

**TIPS & HINTS:**

Chorizo is a cured Spanish sausage made from pork and various spices. It has a strong flavour and a firm texture. Chorizo can be eaten raw but taste better cooked.

# *Much* EASIER ENTERTAINING

YUMMY BBQ'D MUSHIE

# THE "ULTIMATE" BEEF & *Mushroom* BURGER

**Prep: 10 mins   Cook: 15 mins   Serves: 4**

## Ingredients

- 350g beef mince
- 150g Button Mushrooms, chopped
- 2 tbsp chopped tarragon
- 2 tsp Dijon mustard
- 1 egg, lightly whisked
- 100g aged cheddar cheese, sliced
- 4 (100g) rindless bacon rashers
- 4 Portabella Mushrooms
- 4 (80g) burger rolls
- 4 iceberg lettuce leaves, torn
- 2 vine ripened tomatoes, sliced
- ¼ cup whole egg mayonnaise
- ¼ cup tomato chutney

## Method

1. Place mince, mushrooms, tarragon, mustard and egg in the bowl of a food processor and blend until combined. Remove from the bowl, season with salt and pepper and form into 4 patties
2. Pre-heat an oiled char-grill pan or BBQ over medium high heat. Cook burger patty for 3-4 minutes, turn and top with sliced cheese. Cook for a further 3-4 minutes or until cheese is melted and patty is cooked to your liking. Set aside to keep warm
3. Cook bacon for 2-3 minutes each side or until golden and crisp, set aside to keep warm
4. Add mushrooms to pan or BBQ, turning until mushrooms are grilled on both sides and warmed through. Remove from the heat
5. Spread base of mushrooms with mayonnaise, top with iceberg lettuce, tomato, beef patty, bacon and drizzle with tomato chutney to serve

# Much EASIER ENTERTAINING

CRUMBED MUSHIES

# PORTABELLA *Mushroom* FRIES

**Prep: 15 mins    Cook: 10 mins    Serves: 4-6**

## Ingredients

**FRIES**

Vegetable oil, for deep-frying

100g (⅔ cup) plain flour

3 eggs, lighly beaten

2 cups panko breadcrumbs

250g Portabella Mushrooms, stalks trimmed, cut into thin fries

Salt and pepper, to season

**HARISSA YOGHURT**

2 tsp harissa

1 cup Greek-style yoghurt

## Method

**FRIES**

1. Heat enough oil in a large saucepan to come one-third up the sides to 170°C
2. Meanwhile, place the flour, eggs and breadcrumbs into 3 separate wide, shallow bowls
3. Season the flour well with salt and pepper. Dust the mushroom fries in the flour, shaking off any excess, dip into the egg, then coat well in the breadcrumbs
4. In batches, deep-fry the fries for 5 minutes or until golden and cooked. Drain well on paper towel and season with salt

**HARISSA YOGHURT**

1. Mix harissa together with yoghurt. Serve with fries

*Much* **MORE DELICIOUS EVERY DAY**

# Mushroom & Leek Filo Pie

**Prep: 10 mins   Cook: 25 mins   Serves: 4**

## Ingredients

- 20g butter, plus 50g butter, melted
- 2 leeks, trimmed and sliced
- 300g Button Mushrooms, quartered
- 1 garlic clove, crushed
- 100g baby spinach leaves
- 6 eggs, lightly whisked
- ½ cup thickened cream
- ½ cup (50g) grated cheddar cheese
- 50g full fat fresh ricotta cheese, broken into pieces
- 2 tsp finely grated lemon rind, plus lemon wedges to serve
- 6 sheets filo pastry

## Method

1. Preheat oven to 200°C fan-forced. Heat 20g butter in a large deep frying pan over high heat. Add the leeks and mushrooms and cook for 3-5 minutes or until browned. Add garlic and cook, stirring for 1 minute. Remove from the heat and stir in spinach leaves, until just wilted. Set aside to cool slightly
2. Whisk eggs and cream in a medium size bowl. Add mushroom mixture, cheese and lemon rind. Season with salt and pepper
3. Lay a 50cm long piece of baking paper on the bench. Top with 1 layer of filo pastry, brush with melted butter, top with another sheet of filo pastry and repeat until all pastry sheets are layered on top of each other
4. Heat an oiled large deep frying pan with oven-proof handle over medium heat. Lift baking paper sheet into frying pan, easing down the edges into the pan. Stir egg and mushroom mixture and pour into pastry case
5. Scrunch the pastry edges over the mushroom mixture. Transfer to the oven and cook for 20-25 minutes or until the egg is set and the pastry is golden
6. Serve with lemon wedges and freshly ground black pepper

**TIPS & HINTS:**

Always use fresh refrigerated filo pastry, anything from the freezer will be brittle and break easily

# Mushroom VEGGIE BURGERS

Prep: **10 mins**   Cook: **10 mins**   Serves: **4**

## Ingredients

- ⅓ cup (50ml) thick Greek-style yoghurt
- 1 tbsp lemon juice
- 1 tbsp finely chopped mint leaves
- 2 garlic cloves, crushed
- 3 tbsp olive oil
- 200g Button Mushrooms, trimmed and halved
- ½ tsp ground cumin
- ½ tsp ground coriander
- 400g can chickpeas, rinsed and drained
- 1 carrot, peeled and coarsely grated
- ¼ cup (10g) parsley leaves
- Plain flour, for dusting
- 4 (80g each) Ciabatta rolls, halved
- 4 canned baby beets, sliced
- 1 Lebanese cucumber, sliced into ribbons
- 4 butter lettuce leaves

## Method

1. Combine yoghurt, lemon juice, 1 garlic clove and mint in a small bowl, set aside
2. Heat 1 tablespoon olive oil in a medium frying pan over medium high heat, add mushrooms. Cook for 4 minutes, add remaining garlic, cumin and coriander and cook for a further 1 minute or until mushrooms are fragrant and golden. Allow to cool slightly
3. Place chickpea, carrot, parsley and mushroom mixture in the bowl of a food processor and blend until just combined. Shape into 4 patties, dust in flour
4. Heat remaining oil in a large frying pan. Cook patties for 3-4 minutes each side or until crisp and golden
5. Place base of rolls on serving platter, spread evenly with yoghurt, top with lettuce, mushroom patty, cucumber and top of roll to serve

**TIPS & HINTS:**

Drizzle with chilli oil for an extra kick!

*Much* **MORE DELICIOUS EVERY DAY** •

# Mushroom & Char Siu Pork Stir Fry

**Prep: 10 mins   Cook: 15 mins   Serves: 4**

## Ingredients

- ⅓ cup char siu sauce
- 2 tsp Chinese five spiced powder
- 2 tbsp soy sauce
- 1 tbsp peanut oil
- 500g pork fillet (tenderloin), thinly sliced
- 400g Button Mushrooms
- ½ cup (125ml) water
- 2 bunches (480g) gailan (Chinese broccoli), trimmed and cut into 5cm lengths
- 2 green onions, thinly sliced on the angle
- 1 tbsp black sesame seeds
- Rice noodles, to serve

## Method

1. Cook rice noodles according to packet instructions. Set aside and keep warm
2. Place char siu and five spice powder in a small jug and mix to combine. Spread 2 tablespoons of mixture onto pork. Add soy sauce to remaining mixture, stir to combine
3. Heat oil in large deep frying pan over medium heat. Add pork, and stir-fry for 6-8 minutes, turning until browned all over. Add mushrooms, cook stirring for 2 minutes, until golden. Add remaining marinade and water to pan and bring to a gentle simmer, about 5 minutes. Remove pork and set aside to rest
4. Add gailan to frying pan, cover and cook 2-3 minutes or until tender. Thickly slice pork and serve with mushrooms and gailan and sprinkle with green onion and black sesame. Serve with rice noodles

## Much EASIER ENTERTAINING

# MAPLE ROASTED Mushroom & CARROT SALAD

**Prep:** 10 mins    **Cook:** 35 mins    **Serves:** 4 as a side salad

## Ingredients

**DRESSING**

¼ cup (50ml) maple syrup

2 tbsp olive oil

1 ½ tbsp red wine vinegar

½ tsp chilli flakes

2 bunches (375g each) baby (Dutch) carrots, peeled and trimmed, leaving 1.5cm stalk

1 bunch (375g) baby purple carrots, peeled, halved and trimmed, leaving 1.5cm stalk

400g Swiss Brown Mushrooms, trimmed

¼ cup (40g) roughly chopped hazelnuts

¼ cup (10g) mint leaves

**TO SERVE**

½ cup Greek-style yoghurt

1 - 2 tbsp lemon juice

## Method

**DRESSING**

1. Preheat oven to 200°C fan forced. Combine maple syrup, oil, vinegar and chilli in a small bowl and whisk to combine
2. Place carrots in a large roasting pan, drizzle with 2 tablespoons maple syrup mixture and toss to combine. Roast 10 minutes
3. Add mushrooms and hazelnuts on a baking tray. Drizzle with remaining maple syrup mixture and season with salt and pepper. Roast for 20-25 minutes or until purple carrots are tender

**TO SERVE**

1. Combine yoghurt and lemon juice in a small bowl. Drizzle yoghurt dressing over carrots and serve with mint leaves

**TIPS & HINTS:**

Add rocket leaves and goat curd for a substantial salad.

# Popping candy bark

**Difficulty:** Easy
**Preparation:** 7 mins
**Makes:** 1 sheet (30cm X 30cm)

## Ingredients

- 200g milk or dark chocolate
- 40g Copha
- 40g popping candy

## Method

1. Melt together the Copha and chocolate over a medium heat or microwave on 50% power for 1½ minutes, stirring occasionally until smooth.
2. Spread the mixture in a thin layer onto a tray lined with foil.
3. Whilst the chocolate is still wet, sprinkle evenly with the popping candy.
4. Mark the chocolate with a warm knife into large triangular shards and allow to set in a cool place until required.

**TIP:** Popping candy shards can also be decorated with pure gold leaf (this is edible) for a more glamorous garnish to any dessert platter.

# Honey joys

**Difficulty:** Easy
**Preparation:** 8 - 10 mins
**Cooking:** 10 mins
**Makes:** 18 Honey joys

## Ingredients

- 60g Copha
- 2 tablespoon honey
- ⅓ cup sugar
- 4 cups corn flakes

## Method

1. Pre-heat oven 150°C
2. Melt together the Copha, honey and sugar in a saucepan over low heat, stirring until the sugar has dissolved. Allow mixture to cool slightly.
3. Place the corn flakes into a large mixing bowl, then pour the Copha mixture over. Mix well to coat flakes.
4. Spoon the honey joy mixture into muffin trays lined with paper cases.
5. Bake the honey joys in the pre-heated oven at 150°C for 10 minutes.
6. Remove tray from oven and cool on a wire rack. Honey joys will firm on cooling.
7. When cool, store in an airtight tin.

**TIP:** These honey joys are gluten free. Honey joys can also have sultanas, dried cranberries or chocolate chips added prior to baking.

# Popcorn rocky road

**Difficulty:** Easy
**Preparation:** 15 mins
**Makes:** 20 Squares

## Ingredients

- 100g Copha
- ½ cup cocoa powder
- ½ cup icing sugar
- ½ teaspoon vanilla extract
- 100g white marshmallows, halved
- 50g glace cherries, halved
- 100g caramel popcorn
- white chocolate for decorating

## Method

1. Line the base and sides of a 15 x 30cm slab tin with baking paper.
2. Melt the Copha in a small saucepan over a low heat.
3. Combine the cocoa powder, icing sugar and vanilla in a large bowl. Stir in the Copha until well combined.
4. Fold the marshmallows, glace cherries and caramel popcorn into the Copha mixture and coat all ingredients well.
5. Pour the mixture evenly into the lined tin, press firmly with hands or the back of a flat spoon. Allow to set in a cool place or refrigerate.
6. When the rocky road is set, cut into squares with a warm sharp knife and store in an airtight container until required.

**TIP:**
Setting time 40 minutes. This rocky road is also delicious with the addition of walnuts or toasted slivered almonds. Desiccated coconut may also be added.

# Party snacks

### Fruit Kebabs

**Ingredients**

- Fresh fruit of your choice
- Natural yoghurt
- Wooden skewers

**Method**

1. Cut fruit into pieces roughly the same size.
2. Thread onto skewers, alternating fruit varieties.
3. Serve with yoghurt on the side as a dipping sauce.

## Fun Wraps

### Ingredients

- Wholegrain wraps
- Lettuce, washed and tear into pieces
- Tomatoes, sliced
- Cucumber, sliced into long strips
- Cheddar cheese, cut into long strips
- Cold meat such as ham, chicken or turkey

### Method

1. Layer all ingredients on a wrap
2. Fold up bottom section of wrap, and roll sides in.
3. Wrap in coloured paper covering the bottom half of the wrap, and secure with coloured string or a peg.

# Popping candy hedgehog

**Difficulty:** Easy
**Preparation:** 15 mins / 40 mins refrigeration time
**Cooking:** No cooking required
**Makes:** 16 squares or 12 fingers

## Ingredients

### Hedgehog

- 250g Copha
- 4 tablespoon cocoa powder
- 80g castor sugar
- 1 egg
- 250g shortbread biscuits, roughly chopped
- 50g red jelly lollies, chopped

### Icing

- 30g Copha
- 125g milk chocolate bits
- 50g popping candy pieces

## Method

### Hedgehog

1. Line the base and sides of 30 x 15cm slab tin with baking paper.
2. Combine the cocoa powder and castor sugar in a large bowl and mix well.
3. Melt the Copha in a small saucepan over low heat. Pour the melted Copha into the bowl and mix with the cocoa powder and sugar.
4. Stir in beaten egg.
5. Fold through the biscuit pieces and lollies. Mix together until well combined.
6. Press hedgehog mixture into the lined slab tin.

### Icing

1. Melt together the remaining Copha and chocolate in a bowl. Microwave on 50% power for 1 minute. Stir until well combined.
2. Spread the topping mixture over the hedgehog evenly, sprinkle with popping candy pieces and allow hedgehog to set.
3. Refrigerate for several hours before slicing into squares or fingers using a warm wet knife.
4. Serve as required.

**TIP:**
Refrigeration time 40 minutes. Hedgehogs may be stored in an airtight container for up to 1 month. If you are gluten intolerant, replace shortbread biscuits with rice cookies or popcorn.

# Chocolate crackle popcorn

You can't go wrong with these popcorn sized colourful chocolate crackle balls – the kids will love helping to make and eat them too!

**Difficulty:** Easy
**Preparation:** 30 mins
**Setting Time:** 1 hour
**Makes:** 10 - 15 small popcorn bags or tubs

## Ingredients

- 250g (1 block) Copha
- 200g white chocolate, chopped (not compound)
- 125g (1 cup) icing sugar - sifted
- 60g (½ cup) milk powder
- 4 cups Rice bubbles
- 100g (1 cup) desiccated coconut
- Natural food colouring (multi-colours) - e.g. red, green, yellow, blue

## Method

1. Line 2 flat baking trays with baking paper.
2. Combine white chocolate and Copha in a large bowl. Place over a pot of lightly simmering water. Stir occasionally until melted. Remove from heat.
3. Add the icing sugar, milk powder, rice bubbles and coconut. Stir to combine.
4. Divide mixture evenly into 4 bowls and put a few drops of food colouring in each to get the desired colour you want. Rest the crackle mix for 20 minutes.
5. Pinch off walnut sized pieces and shape into popcorn balls. Place popcorn crackle balls in fridge to set for 1 hour.

## Assembly

1. Mix up the different colour popcorn crackles and divide evenly into popcorn bags or tubs before serving.
2. Store popcorn crackles in an airtight container in the fridge for up to 4 days.

**TIP:** Store popcorn crackles in an airtight container in the fridge for up to 4 days.

# Rainbow tea cake with vanilla frosting & M&M's

Spectacular looking, this colourful birthday treat is easier to make than you think. And you can even make it a day before the party!

**Difficulty:** Medium
**Preparation:** 45 mins
**Cooking:** 30 mins
**Garnishing:** 30 mins
**Makes:** 12 generous slices

## Ingredients

### Tea Cake

- 170g (¾ cup) castor sugar
- 4 eggs
- 150g (1¼ cups) self-raising flour
- 1 tablespoon corn flour
- 15g Copha, melted
- 80ml (⅓ cup) milk
- 3 x 380g M&M's packets, to decorate (replace with Smarties if desired)

### Vanilla Frosting

- 3 cups icing sugar
- 1 cup butter
- 1 teaspoon vanilla extract
- 1 to 2 tablespoon whipping cream

## Method

### Tea Cake

1. Pre heat oven to 170°C (fan forced 150°C) 330°F/300°F. Grease and line an 18cm/7 inch spring form tin with baking grease proof paper.

2. Combine castor sugar and eggs together in an electric mixer and beat for 8 to 10 minutes until pale and creamy and tripled in volume.

3. In a separate bowl, sift together self-raising flour and cornflour 3 times. Sift flours over egg mix and quickly fold through using a spatula, making sure all ingredients are well combined.

4. Melt Copha in microwave or saucepan until fully melted. Warm milk in microwave (on high for 20 seconds). Pour Copha and milk down the side of bowl and fold through the egg and flour mix.

5. Pour final mixture into prepared pan and smooth surface. Bake in oven for 30 minutes or until a skewer inserted into the centre comes out clean. Remove pan from oven.

6. Set cake aside in the pan for 5 - 10 minutes before turning onto a wire rack for 30 minutes to cool completely.

### Vanilla Frosting

1. Using an electric mixer, mix together sugar and butter. Mix on low speed until well blended and then increase speed to medium and beat for another 3 minutes.

2. Add vanilla and cream and continue to beat on medium speed for 1 minute further, adding more cream if needed for spreading consistency.

### Assembly

1. Slice your cake in half horizontally, ensuring you cut as evenly as possible. Place the bottom sponge on a serving plate.
2. Spread vanilla frosting over the base. Place the top cake layer on top of your filling layer.
3. Spread the frosting over the sides and top of the cake evenly.
4. Separate the M&M's by colour. Place a single row of alternating colour M&M's around the base of the cake. Continue to place M&M's row by row up the side of the cake, as per picture. Once the sides are done, continue this same process along the top of the cake.
5. Let frosting set before serving.

**TIP:** Can be stored in fridge for up to 3 days.

# Party snacks

## Monster Apples

### Ingredients

- Granny Smith apples cut into segments
- Natural peanut butter
- Strawberries
- Sunflower seeds (for teeth)
- Mini white marshmallows (for eyes)
- Chocolate chips (for eyes)
- Lollipop sticks

### Method

1. Cut out a slice from each apple segment
2. Spread peanut butter into the cut out of each apple segment
3. Decorate monster mouths with strawberries and sunflower seeds for teeth
4. Place chocolate chips onto mini white marshmallows using a small amount of peanut butter to hold
5. Using a lollipop stick secure the marshmallow eyes onto the apple segment and serve

## Froggy Sandwiches

### Ingredients

- Wholegrain bread
- Ham
- Cheese
- Cucumber
- Olives or cherry tomatoes for eyes
- Toothpicks

### Method

1. Cut bread into circles with a cookie cutter
2. Add cheese and ham to sandwiches
3. Decorate with a cucumber tongue and olives or cherry tomatoes for froggy eyes
4. Secure your froggy sandwiches with toothpicks and serve

# Layered chocolate crackle slice

Crunchy and chocolaty, the kids will want to gobble these up. And we bet you will too!

**Difficulty:** Easy
**Preparation:** 30 mins
**Cooking:** 20 mins
**Makes:** 16 - 20 slices

## Ingredients

### Biscuit Base

- 250g (1 packet) chocolate ripple biscuits
- 100g Copha

### White Chocolate Crackle

- 60g (¼ cup) Copha
- 80g (¾ cup) white chocolate, chopped (not compound)
- 65g (½ cup) icing sugar
- 25g (1 cup) rice bubbles
- 30g (¼ cup) milk powder
- 20g (⅓ cup) desiccated coconut

### Dark Chocolate Crackle

- 60g (¼ cup) Copha
- 80g (¾ cup) dark cooking chocolate (chopped)
- 65g (½ cup) icing sugar
- 25g (1 cup) rice bubbles
- 2 tablespoons cocoa powder
- 20g (⅓ cup) desiccated coconut
- ¼ cup pouring cream

## Method

### Biscuit Base

1. Grease and line with baking paper a 25cm x 16cm x 2 ½cm (10in x 6in x 1in) baking tray. Make sure the paper has a 2cm over hang.
2. Melt Copha in microwave on high or in saucepan until fully melted. Using a food processor, crush biscuits until they resemble fine breadcrumbs.
3. Mix melted Copha and biscuit crumbs together. Then press biscuit mix into baking tray firmly, using the back of a spoon if necessary. Put in the fridge to set for 10 to 15 minutes.

### White chocolate crackle layer

1. In a large bowl, combine together white chocolate and Copha. Place bowl over a pot of lightly simmering water. Stir occasionally until melted. Remove from heat.
2. Add icing sugar, rice bubbles, milk powder and coconut to the bowl. Stir to combine.
3. Pour crackle mix over the biscuit base and spread evenly. Put back in the fridge to set.

### Dark chocolate layer

1. In a large bowl combine dark chocolate and Copha. Place over a pot of lightly simmering water. Stir occasionally until melted. Remove from heat.
2. Add icing sugar, rice bubbles, cocoa powder and coconut to the bowl. Stir to combine. Pour dark chocolate crackle mix over white chocolate layer and biscuit base and spread evenly. Put back in the fridge to set.

# Mini red velvet cupcakes

Make these mini-cupcakes for something fun and yummy to add to the party table. And the smaller portion sizes should keep the adults happy too!

**Difficulty:** Medium
**Preparation:** 30 mins
**Cooking:** 20 mins
**Makes:** 12 standard or 24 mini cupcakes

## Ingredients

### Cupcakes

- 225g (1¼ cup) self-raising flour
- 25g (¼ cup) cocoa powder
- 150g (½ cup) castor sugar
- 60g (¼ cup) diced Copha
- 2 eggs
- 1 teaspoon vanilla essence
- 125ml (½ cup) buttermilk
- 1 tablespoon red food colouring
- 1 teaspoon bi-carbonate of soda
- 1 tablespoon white vinegar
- Colourful sprinkles/100s and 1000s (for decoration)
- 1 small packet of Smarties (for decoration)

### Copha cream cheese frosting

- 250g (1 cup) softened cream cheese
- 125g (½ cup) softened Copha
- 250g (2 cups) icing sugar
- 1 teaspoon vanilla essence

## Method

### Cupcakes

1. Pre-heat oven to 180°C (fan forced 160° C) 350°F/320°F. Line a standard 12-hole cupcake/muffin pan with paper cases for standard sized cupcakes, or a 24-hole pan for mini-cupcakes.
2. Sift together self-raising flour and cocoa powder. Soften Copha in microwave in 30 second increments until just soft enough to beat.
3. Cream Copha and castor sugar using an electric mixer; adding eggs one at a time.
4. Combine vanilla essence, buttermilk and food colouring in a bowl, microwave on high for 30 seconds. Turn mixer to low speed. Add flour mix and buttermilk in batches.
5. In a small bowl, stir together the bi-carbonate soda and vinegar. Add to the cupcake batter. Divide batter equally into the prepared pan and bake for 15 - 20 minutes or until skewer inserted into the centre comes out clean.
6. Set aside for 5 - 10 minutes in the pan before turning onto a wire rack for cooling.

### Copha Cream Cheese Frosting

1. Soften Copha in microwave in 30 second increments until just soft enough to beat.
2. Pre-warm the outside of your electric mixer bowl with running hot water (to keep Copha soft). Add Copha, cream cheese, icing sugar and vanilla essence to your bowl and beat until well combined.

### Assembly

1. Fill a piping bag fitted with a 2cm nozzle with frosting.
2. Pipe swirls over the cupcakes.
3. Decorate your cupcakes with 100s and 1000s and smarties.

**TIP:**
Serve at room temperature; best to take out from the fridge 1 hour before serving. Can be stored in an airtight container in the fridge for up to 3 days.

# Party snacks

## Berry Smoothies

### Ingredients

- Raspberries or strawberries, stems removed
- Bananas, peeled and roughly chopped
- Natural yoghurt
- Milk or coconut water

### Method

1. Add all ingredients to a blender, and process until smooth. Adjust quantities of fruit and liquid to get desired consistency.

## Smiley Toasts

### Ingredients

- Wholegrain bread
- Cream cheese
- Cherry tomatoes, sliced (for eyes)
- Carrots, peeled and sliced (for nose)
- Cucumber, cut into semi-circles (for mouth)
- Spring onions, sliced into thin strips (for eyelashes)

### Method

1. Toast the bread
2. Spread with cream cheese
3. Decorate with chopped vegetables as desired. Use your imagination!

# Mini chocolate mudcakes

Make these mini mudcakes for something fun and yummy to add to the party table. And the smaller portion sizes should keep the adults happy too!

**Difficulty:** Medium
**Preparation:** 40 mins
**Cooking:** 45 mins
**Makes:** 12

## Ingredients

### Mudcakes

- 250g (1 block) diced Copha
- 250g chopped milk cooking chocolate (can also substitute for dark cooking chocolate if desired)
- 500g (1¼ cups) firmly packed brown sugar
- 4 eggs
- 125ml (½ cup) sour cream
- 300g (2⅓ cups) plain flour
- 1 teaspoon baking powder
- 60g (⅓ cup) cocoa powder
- Jelly lollies to garnish

### Chocolate Ganache

- 180g chopped milk or dark cooking chocolate
- 80ml (⅓ cup) thickened cream (plus extra for serving)

## Method

### Mudcakes

1. Pre heat oven to 140°C (fan forced 120° C) 280°F/240°F. Lightly grease and double line a 21cm/8in spring form pan making sure the paper is 5cm/2in above the rim.

2. Combine cooking chocolate and brown sugar together in a bowl. Place bowl over a pot of lightly simmering water to melt. Stir occasionally until fully melted. Remove from heat and set aside for 5 minutes.

3. Melt Copha in the microwave or saucepan until fully melted. Add melted chocolate. Whisk eggs in one at a time followed by sour cream.

4. Combine plain flour, baking powder and cocoa powder and sift over Copha mix. Stir through until well combined.

5. Divide cake mix equally into muffin pan and bake in the oven for 45 minutes or until a skewer inserted into the centre comes out clean. Remove pan from oven. Set cake aside in the pan for 5 - 10 minutes before turning onto a wire rack for 30 minutes or until cooled completely.

### Chocolate Ganache

1. In a medium sized saucepan, bring cream to boil over medium heat.

2. Remove from heat, add chocolate and stir until combined and glossy. Set aside to cool.

### Assembly

1. Spoon ganache mixture over the top of each mini-cake.
2. Top with a jelly lolly.
3. Let frosting set before serving.

**TIP:**
If refrigerated, bring to room temperature before serving. Can be stored in an air-tight container in the fridge for up to 3 days.

# Chocolate crackles

Chocolate crackles are a favourite for kids parties. So quick and easy to make, this sweet and crunchy delight is bound to please your guests, no matter what the age!

**Difficulty:** Easy
**Preparation:** 10 mins
**Makes:** 10 Crackles

## Ingredients

- Dark chocolate crackle
- 250g (1 block) Copha
- 125g (1 cup) Icing sugar
- 60g (½ cup) Cocoa powder
- 4 cups Rice bubbles
- 100g (1 cup) Desiccated coconut

## Method

1. Line a standard 12 cup muffin tray with paper cases.
2. Melt Copha in microwave on high or in a saucepan until fully melted. Mix rice bubbles, icing sugar, cocoa powder and desiccated coconut in a large bowl. Add in the melted Copha, and stir to combine.
3. Spoon crackle mix evenly into the prepared muffin cups. Place in fridge for 1 hour to set.

**TIP:** Can be stored in an airtight container in the fridge for up to 4 days.

# Coconut ice

This delicious no-bake coconut ice recipe is simple and quick to make and is an old favourite that the kids will love.

**Difficulty:** Easy
**Preparation:** 15 mins
**Makes:** 40 Squares

## Ingredients

- 250g Copha
- 1 kg icing sugar, sifted
- 500g desiccated coconut
- 3 egg whites
- 1 tsp vanilla essence
- Pink food colouring

**TIP:** This coconut ice is gluten-free.

## Method

**Melt N Mix – no baking required!**

1. Line a 30cm x 15cm slab tin with baking paper.
2. In a large bowl combine the sifted icing sugar and coconut. Mix well. Make a large well in the centre.
3. Melt the Copha in a small saucepan over a low heat; remove and add the vanilla essence. Pour Copha into the icing sugar and coconut mixture.
4. Whisk the egg whites until foamy but not stiff. Stir the egg whites into the mixture until well combined.
5. Divide the mixture in half. Press half the mixture into the slab tin; to make the mixture even press with a flat-based glass. Refrigerate until firm.
6. Add a few drops of pink colour to the remaining mixture and knead well to give the coconut ice an even colour.
7. Press the pink mixture over the white coconut ice and press firmly. Refrigerate coconut ice until firm.
8. Using a warm knife or shaped cutter cut the coconut ice into the required shapes. Decorate and serve as required.

# a custard erole

...elebrations, these divine tasting profiteroles ...custard filling will get everyone in the ...pirit!

Medium
15 mins
20 mins
18

**ts**

...p) water
...diced Copha
...) plain flour

...oking chocolate,
...an also substitute
...oking chocolate)
...chocolate,

...balls or sprinkles

**Kahlúa custard filling**
- 250ml (1 cup) thickened cream
- 250ml (1 cup) milk
- 80ml (⅓ cup) Kahlúa
- 1 teaspoon vanilla bean paste
- 6 egg yolks
- 60g (⅓ cup) castor sugar
- 4 tablespoon corn flour
- ¼ cup pouring cream

**TIP:**
Store in an airtight container in the fridge for up to 3 days.

to 220°C (fan forced 200°C)
ightly grease and line 2 baking
chment paper.

er and Copha in a medium-sized
ng to the boil. Reduce heat
ur and stir to combine, stirring
r 3 to 5 minutes until mixture
the pan and forms a mass.

heat and set aside for 5 minutes.
ric mixer add eggs in one at a
well between each addition on
d. The mix should be stiff and
d up on the tip of a spoon.

oon, spoon 18 walnut sized balls
acing 6cm apart. Alternatively,
poon mix into a piping bag fitted
nozzle and use that for piping
y. Bake for 10 minutes, rotate
uce heat to 200°C/180°C.

ng puffs for a further 10 minutes,
d springy to the touch.

e tray for 5–10 minutes. Then
re rack to cool completely.

### Kahlúa custard filling

1. Combine cream, milk, Kahlúa and vanilla bean paste in a saucepan. Bring to boil over medium heat. Remove from stove.

2. In a bowl whisk together egg yolks, castor sugar and corn flour. Slowly add cream, whisking continuously, until thoroughly combined.

3. Pour mix back into the saucepan and return to a low heat. Stir continuously until the custard thickens and coats the back of the spoon. Remove from heat, set aside to cool. Cover with cling film and put in the fridge until ready to use.

## Assembly

1. Put Kahlúa custard in a piping bag fitted with a 5mm nozzle.

2. Make a small hole in the bottom of the cream puff with a sharp knife and pipe custard in.

3. Melt the milk chocolate and add in pouring cream in batches and mix thoroughly till smooth.

4. Melt white chocolate separately.

5. Spoon milk chocolate mix over profiterole. Allow milk chocolate mix to set before drizzling white chocolate over profiterole, as per image.

6. Decorate with silver edible balls or sprinkles.

# [Glute]n free [mini] fruitcakes

[Bring the fl]avours of Christmas to your table with these [delicious gl]uten free mini fruitcakes.

Medium
30 mins
25 mins
12

**TIP:** Serve at room temperature; we suggest taking out from the fridge 1 hour before serving.

### [Ingredien]ts

- [...] raisins
- [...] chopped
- [...] currants
- [...] chopped dates
- [...] mixed peel
- [...] orange juice
- [...] brandy
- [...] diced Copha
- [...] firmly packed [suga]r
- [...] sour cream

- 2 eggs
- 150g (1¼ cup) gluten free plain flour
- 75g (⅔ cup) gluten free self-raising flour
- 1 teaspoon ground cinnamon
- ½ teaspoon mixed spice

**For garnishing**
- 1 cup fresh or preserved pitted cherries
- 3 tablespoon castor sugar
- 1 cup pre-mix custard

e the night before. Combine
uit, orange juice and brandy
owl, cover and leave to
t.

to 170°C (fan forced 150°C)
ightly grease 2 six-cup

microwave or saucepan until
Whisk together melted Copha
gar, add sour cream and whisk
t a time.

lain flour, self-raising flour,
xed spice and nutmeg in
wl. Fold through the Copha
oaked fruit, and stir through.

equally into the prepared
e for 25 to 30 minutes, or until
ted into the centre comes out
ve pans from oven. Set cakes
an for 5 – 10 minutes before
a wire rack to cool completely.

rries and sugar in a saucepan.
cherries, add 50ml of water into
; if using preserved cherries,
he syrup.

e boil over medium heat.
eat to low and simmer for
until liquid has reduced
a syrup.

### Assembly

1. Make custard according to instructions on packet.
2. Place cakes onto serving plate; warm in microwave if desired.
3. Drizzle custard over cake and serve with cherry compote on the side.

# ve red velvet kes

et memories this festive season with these
Christmas cupcakes.

Medium
30 mins
20 mins
12 standard or 24 mini-cupcakes

ts

p) self-raising flour
 cocoa powder
) castor sugar
 diced Copha

 vanilla essence
p) buttermilk
n red food

 bicarbonate of

n white vinegar
 balls or sprinkles
ion)

### Cream Cheese Frosting
- 250g (1 cup) softened cream cheese
- 125g (½ cup) softened Copha
- 250g (2 cups) icing sugar
- 1 teaspoon vanilla essence

**TIP:** Serve at room temperature; we suggest taking out from the fridge 1 hour before serving.

to 180°C (fan forced
320°F. Line a standard
ke/muffin pan with paper
dard sized cupcakes,
an for mini-cupcakes.

elf-raising flour and cocoa
n Copha in microwave in
rements until just soft
at.

a and castor sugar using an
adding eggs one at a time.

lla essence, buttermilk and food
bowl, microwave on high for 30
mixer to low speed. Add flour
rmilk in batches.

l, stir together the bi-carbonate
gar. Add to the cup cake batter.

equally into the prepared pan
15 – 20 minutes or until skewer
he centre comes out clean.
– 10 minutes in the pan before
wire rack for cooling.

### Cream Cheese Frosting

1. Soften Copha in microwave in 30 second increments until just soft enough to beat.

2. Prewarm the outside of your electric mixer bowl with running hot water (to keep Copha soft). Add Copha, cream cheese, icing sugar and vanilla essence to your bowl and beat until well combined.

### Assembly

1. Fill a piping bag fitted with a 2cm nozzle with frosting.

2. Pipe swirls over the cup cakes.

3. Decorate your cupcakes with sprinkles, edible glitter or edible pearls.

# tmas
# late mudcake

asions deserve to be celebrated in style.
onderfully decadent Christmas chocolate
ultimate in indulgence!

Medium
40 mins
2 – 2½ hours
12 to 16 slices

## ts

ck) diced Copha
ed milk cooking
can also
r dark cooking
desired)
ps) firmly packed

p) sour cream
ps) plain flour
baking powder
cocoa

### Chocolate Ganache

- 180g chopped milk or dark cooking chocolate
- 80ml (⅓ cup) thickened cream (plus extra for serving)

**TIP:**
If refrigerated, bring to room temperature before serving. Can be stored in an air-tight container in the fridge for up to 3 days.

to 140°C (fan forced 120°C)
ightly grease and double line
ring form pan making sure
cm/2in above the rim.

king chocolate and brown
r in a bowl. Place bowl over
 simmering water to melt. Stir
until fully melted. Remove from
aside for 5 minutes.

 the microwave or saucepan
ed. Add melted chocolate.
 one at a time followed by

 flour, baking powder and
er and sift over Copha mix.
til well combined.

 into the prepared pan and
ven for 2 – 2½ hours or until a
d into the centre comes out
ve pan from oven.

e in the pan for 5 – 10 minutes
 onto a wire rack for 30 minutes
d completely.

### Chocolate Ganache

1. In a medium sized saucepan, bring cream to boil over medium heat.

2. Remove from heat, add chocolate and stir until combined and glossy. Set aside to cool.

### Assembly

1. Spoon ganache mixture into a piping bag fitted with a 1.5cm fluted nozzle.

2. Pipe rosettes over the top of the cake.

3. Allow ganache to set.

4. Serve with pouring cream.

# balls

Easy
20 mins / 40 mins setting time
No cooking required
16

### To Coat
- 100g dark chocolate
- 30g Copha

### Coatings
- cocoa powder
- chocolate sprinkles
- ground praline
- shredded coconut

**TIP:**
, milk or white
te may be used as
ng for Rum Balls.
ake crumbs may
e used in place of
ake crumbs.

...owave safe bowl melt together
...chocolate on medium power
..., stirring occasionally until
...oth.

...crumbs, almonds and rum into
... mixture. Allow to cool.

...ture into 16 walnut sized balls
... rum balls onto a tray lined
...aper. Refrigerate until firm.

...ining Copha and chocolate
...smooth.

...oo stick into the centre of each
...ip into the chocolate mixture.
...ll into the chosen coating and

...emaining balls. Serve as required.

# idual gluten tiramisu

ooohs and aaahs with this decadent tiramisu, topped with cream and shavings.

Medium
1½ hours
20 mins
6 to 8

**TIP:** For best results make this the night before serving. Works well with glasses with 180ml – 250ml capacity.

### ts

**r Biscuits**
- diced Copha
- rated
- castor sugar
- vanilla essence
- gluten free
- gluten free our
- gluten free der

ving sizes are endent on size erving glass, how generous portions are.

**Mascarpone cream**
- 500ml (2 cups) strong black coffee (hot)
- 125ml (½ cup) marsala
- 100g (½ cup) castor sugar
- 4 eggs separated
- 160g (¾ cup) mascarpone
- 160ml (¾ cup) thickened cream
- cocoa powder for dusting
- 50g dark chocolate, grated
- maraschino cherries to decorate.

Transfer mix to a large bowl, then fold the mascarpone gently through one third at a time; keep in the fridge until ready to use.

3. Beat cream using an electric mixer until soft peaks form; keep in the fridge until ready to use.

4. Beat egg whites using an electric mixer, until soft peaks form. Slowly add the remaining castor sugar and whisk for a further 2 minutes.

5. Take mascarpone mix and whipped cream from fridge; fold whipped cream gently through one third at a time into the mascarpone mix. Then fold in egg whites gently one third at a time. Keep refrigerated until ready to assemble.

### Assembly

1. Each glass will hold three biscuits and ½ a cup of mascarpone cream.

2. To assemble the tiramisu, cut the biscuits into thirds. Dip four pieces of biscuit at a time into the coffee mixture, squeeze out the excess liquid and arrange in the bottom of the glass.

3. Spoon two tablespoons of mascarpone cream over the biscuit making a smooth layer.

4. Continue the process until the glass is full, finishing off with a layer of cream. (There should be two layers of biscuit and two layers of cream)

5. Dust with cocoa powder and sprinkle grated chocolate over the top, then finish with a maraschino cherry.

Serve immediately or keep refrigerated until ready to serve.

# ed chocolate
# le slice

ith the kids in the kitchen and make these
mas delights to give as gifts to friends and
s a treat for yourself!

Easy
30 mins
25 mins
16 to 20

**ts**

**ate Crackle**
- Copha
- white chocolate, ot compound)
- icing sugar
- rice bubbles
- milk powder
- desiccated

**Dark Chocolate Crackle**
- 60g (¼ cup) Copha
- 80g (¾ cup) dark cooking chocolate (chopped)
- 65g (½ cup) icing sugar
- 25g (1 cup) Rice bubbles
- 2 tablespoons cocoa powder
- 20g (⅓ cup) desiccated coconut

**Biscuit Base**
- 250g (1 packet) chocolate ripple biscuits
- 100g Copha

e crackle
squares.
s can be
airtight
he fridge
days

139

ne with baking paper a
 2½ cm (10in x 6in x 1in)
ake sure the paper has
ang.

 microwave on high or in
l fully melted. Using a food
sh biscuits until they resemble
mbs.

opha and biscuit crumbs together.
cuit mix into baking tray firmly,
k of a spoon if necessary. Put in
et for 10 to 15 minutes.

 crackle layer

vl, combine together white
d Copha. Place bowl over a
mmering water. Stir occasionally
emove from heat.

ar, rice bubbles, milk powder
to the bowl. Stir to combine.

mix over the biscuit base and
. Put back in the fridge to set.

### Dark chocolate layer

1. In a large bowl combine dark chocolate and Copha. Place over a pot of lightly simmering water. Stir occasionally until melted. Remove from heat.

2. Add icing sugar, rice bubbles, cocoa powder and coconut to the bowl. Stir to combine. Pour dark chocolate crackle mix over white chocolate layer and biscuit base and spread evenly. Put back in the fridge to set.

### Assembly

1. Once set, slice crackle into 16 to 20 squares.

# and dark late crackles

stmas without chocolate crackles!
ds will love helping out too because it's
make chocolate crackles – no cooking
equired!

Easy
30 mins
1 hour
24 crackles

ts

olate Crackle
ck) Copha
) icing sugar
) cocoa powder
gg's Rice
ereal
) desiccated

White Chocolate Crackle
- 250g (1 block) Copha
- 125g (1 cup) icing sugar
- 60g (½ cup) milk powder
- 4 cups Kellogg's Rice Bubbles® cereal
- 100g (1cup) desiccated coconut

dard muffin tray with 12 muffin liners

a in microwave on high. Combine
s, icing sugar, cocoa powder and
a bowl, add melted Copha, stir
e.

kle mix evenly over the dark
crackle. Put in fridge for
t.

**TIP:**
Store crackles in an airtight container in the fridge for up to 4 days.

## Assembly
1. Put a decorative collar around the crackle to serve.
2. Serve.

# Christmas

A Christmas favourite everyone loves and so [easy to make]. Don't forget White Christmas is a great [gift idea]. Package squares in clear cellophane [and tie] with colourful ribbons.

- Easy
- 15 mins
- 15 mins
- 24

- [Kellogg']s Rice Bubbles®
- [desicca]ted coconut
- [icing su]gar, sifted
- 1 cup powdered milk
- 1 packaged, dried mixed fruit
- Glacé cherries for topping

[Combine dry] ingredients in a mixing bowl.

[Melt sl]owly over low heat.

[P]our onto dry ingredients.

[Quick]ly spoon into paper patty cases [or into] a lamington tin.

[Allow to se]t (about 15 minutes), then store [in refriger]ator.

[Cut into squa]rs, top with glacé cherries and serve.

www.ingramcontent.com/pod-product-compliance
Lightning Source LLC
Chambersburg PA
CBHW081414080526
44589CB00016B/2536